What Reviewers Are Saying About *Chiquita's Cocoon*

"Highly recommended. Straight talk and sound advice characterize this impressive self-help guide for the Latina Woman."
—*Booklist*

"It has many messages . . . [and] has found admirers throughout the state."
—*Los Angeles Times*

"Flores has spun a bold yet bubbly manual to help Latinas . . . evolve into women who are free, strong, secure, aware and happy."
—*Sacramento Bee*

"*Chiquita's Cocoon* is everywoman's cocoon . . . the book's message crosses cultural and economic lines."
—*The Fresno Women's Network Newsletter*

"Bettina Flores . . . woman on a mission."
—*El Paisano Daily*
Rio Hondo College

"The twelve-chapter book has an important message for all Latinas."
—*La Opinión*

"A classic! Gutsy Latina author Bettina Flores is tossing a smart wallop to society with her first book, *Chiquita's Cocoon*."
—*Napa County Record*

What People Are Saying About *Chiquita's Cocoon*

"Powerful! A life-changing book."
—RUTH BARRIOS, Sacramento, Cal.

"Wow! I never looked at my life this way."
—RACHEL ALVAREZ, Fort Dix, N.J.

"If you're tired of living in a 'What José wants, José gets' world, *Chiquita's Cocoon* is for you."
—ROSA FLORES, Fresno, Cal.

"Anyone living her life dictated by cultural traditions which are outdated (because family, other relatives, friends, church and society say they must) needs this book."
—OLIVIA SANCHEZ, Los Angeles, Cal.

"It's about time."
—BEATRIZ LEWIS DIAZ, El Paso, Tex.

"I carry the Bible in one hand and *Chiquita's Cocoon* in the other."
—LAURA ETEGORIAN, Hanford, Cal.

What Educators Are Saying About *Chiquita's Cocoon*

"*Chiquita's Cocoon* makes a very important contribution to the self-esteem of Latinas."
—HOWARD HOMLER, M.D., director, Health Education
Network, Sacramento, Cal.

"It's about time someone tells it as it is! Bravo! I am so enthusiastic about your book that I am going to [use it] for my ESL [English as a Second Language] students. Believe me, they need to read it!"
—TERE TIBBETTS, teacher, South Lake Tahoe, Cal.

"The book has the potential to positively revolutionize the thinking of young women inside and outside the Latino community. [It will] serve as part of the core reading for the counseling staff and interns . . . in the university counseling service.
—DR. RALPH DAWSON, coordinator, California State University,
Los Angeles, Cal.

"We are so excited about the students' reactions to your book and their new awareness of themselves. We plan to use the book in class."
—SALLIE BROWN, professor of English,
El Camino Community College, Torrance, Cal.

"*Chiquita's Cocoon* has been adopted for Anthropology 354—The Family in Cross-Cultural Perspective."
—MONICA UDVARDY, instructor, Department of Anthropology,
University of Kentucky

"Even though I'm educated, it made me open my eyes, because those cultural obstacles on a personal and professional level still come back to haunt me."
—JULIE CHAVEZ BAYLES, teacher, Montebello High,
Montebello, Cal.

What Feminists Are Saying About *Chiquita's Cocoon*

Chiquita's Cocoon

Bettina R. Flores

Chiquita's Cocoon

The Latina Woman's Guide to Greater Power,
Love, Money, Status and Happiness

Villard Books
New York
1994

Grateful acknowledgment is made to the following for permission to reprint previously
published material:
GREENWOOD PRESS: Excerpt from *Dictionary of Mexican-American History* by Matt S.
Meier and Feliciano Rivera (pp. 86–88). Copyright © 1981 by Matt S. Meier and
Feliciano Rivera. Reprinted by permission.
ELISA A. MARTINEZ: "Having the Choice of Who to Be" by Elisa A. Martinez. Reprinted
by permission of the author.

Library of Congress Cataloging-in-Publication Data
Flores, Bettina.
Chiquita's cocoon: the Latina woman's guide to
greater power, love, money, status and happiness / by
Bettina R. Flores.
p. cm.
ISBN 0-679-75044-4 (alk. paper)
1. Feminism—United States. 2. Hispanic American women.
3. Mexican American women. 4. Self-actualization (Psychology)
I. Title.
HQ1421.F58 1994
305.48'86872—dc20   93-25981

Manufactured in the United States of America on acid-free paper

9 8 7 6 5 4 3 2
First Edition

To Alfredo, my husband, mi amor y compañero de mi vida.

To Ruth, my sister, who stood by me from the first page of the first draft to the last page of the finished book.

And in memory of Josie Coronado, our beloved sister.

Preface

Chiquita's Cocoon is Everywoman's cocoon. A woman in California wrote that in a story about this book.

I hadn't really realized it until I, a Latina author and self-publisher, had sold nearly twenty thousand copies of *Chiquita's Cocoon* anywhere I could, from baby showers to book conventions.

But each week, brave letters and phone calls would come (they still do) from readers everywhere saying, I'm white, not Latina, and your book is telling my story. I'm Asian; I've lived every bit of your book. I'm Cuban and, boy, do I relate. I'm Puerto Rican, but your mother sounds just like my mother. You know, Bettina, African American women also experience cultural oppression. Jewish women chimed in, too.

Then I spoke at a national conference for school desegregation, where many ethnic groups were represented. After my lecture the master of ceremonies enthusiastically remarked, "Here's the key, folks. When you read *Chiquita's Cocoon* just replace the word *Latina* with your identity. Believe me, everyone can relate!" That day, I heard one cocoon story after another—from non-Latinos! (A cocoon story is one that relates a person's escape from within the stifling confines of his or her cultural cocoon.)

It's so true—cultural oppression is universal, particularly when it comes to women.

The subject of cultural oppression is a sensitive one and many people are not yet ready to hear or face it. I understand this. A self-defense mechanism called denial comes into play when reality causes emotional pain. So I'm offering this short discussion in a spirit of respect for cultural diversity. Keep in mind, the reasons for acting "culturally" are complex and this is only one tiny little book. On the other hand, there's nothing our minds can't grasp when we really want to.

I am both honored and excited that *Chiquita's Cocoon* is touching the minds and hearts of women (and men) from so many diversified cultures. With all we've yet to accomplish for women as a whole, we should be careful not to buy into too much separateness. It is equally important to realize that culture is not a static phenomenon; in fact it changes with every generation. Ethnic immigrants to the United States give birth to new Americans, and these new Americans may take the opportunity to mix with other ethnics. It is my hope that in the new cultural mix we will retain the good aspects of our individual cultures and reject the bad, the outdated, and the oppressive ones—especially those that affect women.

We all have our history and pain and promises. I still shudder when I see a painting of the Spanish conquistadores who ravished Mexico. I'm sure Cuban Americans have a lot to say about the Cuban revolution, Castro, Batista, and the Bay of Pigs invasion. Puerto Rican Americans have their issues of statehood and their feelings about cultural integration with the United States. Many

Japanese Americans were deeply injured by their internment after Pearl Harbor. Dr. Martin Luther King, Jr.'s cause will never be forgotten, nor the Holocaust or any other devastating crisis where human rights are trampled. I am mourning the loss of this century's greatest farmworker leader, Cesar Chavez, who voluntarily dedicated his life to the well-being of migrant workers everywhere.

Naturally, our attitudes, interests and beliefs are different because we are different. However, because we cannot and should not live in the past, each of us needs to understand our cultural background to learn how deeply it affects our life. Every woman should understand how she has been socialized so she can decide whether she wants to follow along the same path as her mother or grandmother or to make changes now. Today, women emerging from the American ethnic mix have the opportunity to define the new cultural directions of a society that has previously been dominated by men. This, of course, can only be accomplished when women become aware and courageous enough to tackle the perpetrators of cultural oppression, whether they be men or women, in their families, jobs and social relations.

We all possess ethnic pride. It is reflected in our individual language, music, art, folklore and food and often in deep loyalty to specific religions. We celebrate holidays and milestones in life with certain customs and traditions that we pass on to our children. Ethnic pride is definitely beneficial because it enhances one's self-esteem—and having diversified cultures certainly makes for a much more interesting and delightful world to live in.

Likewise, we have our Jewish neighborhoods, our barrios, our Spanish Harlems, our Little Havanas, our Chinatowns, our ghettos and our West Side stories. We commonly hear: I'm from the South. I grew up in the Midwest. I'm a Texan. California is the only place to live. And many generations, from the *Mayflower* to the Mexican border, still hold sacred the sagas of their journey *to* the United States and their difficult lives in the "early days."

Cultures also have a self-governing structure or a social order system. Basically, when the father or other male rules the family, it's called a patriarchy; when a woman functions as the head of the household, it's a matriarchy. Worldwide, most cultures are patriarchies with men having significant, if not total, power over their community members, whether immediate family or the larger society. (We've only to look around us to know who's running the show.)

Women, of course, have been taught and conditioned to support the power and position of their men. And, ladies, if we are to be honest with ourselves, we'll admit that we are the breeders of more of the same! Male dominance (machismo) permeates many cultures, historically and habitually oppressing the rights of women. Therefore, when it comes to the cultural oppression of women and the subject of machismo, the mind-set is pretty much the same even in culturally diverse groups. This is how *Chiquita's Cocoon* becomes Everywoman's cocoon.

Many women have told me they relate to *Chiquita's Cocoon* because it's written from a woman's point of view and with a woman's compassion. They say I've shown them the outdated and harmful so-called cultural values that control women's lives. From the kitchen to the bedroom to the workplace, I've exposed those mind-twisting, power-playing, macho-tripping, and belittling innuendos that on the surface appear as everyday chitchat but that in reality deny women human dignity!

In *Chiquita's Cocoon* I've spared no one—myself, my mother, family, husband, church, government, society, and least of all, my cultural upbringing.

Along with all this heavy stuff, however, my readers tell me *Chiquita's Cocoon* made them laugh and cry. Some even said a miracle happened. Most say, "It changed my life." I'm so grateful that the book's message can make culturally conditioned women think, and dream and dare to reach for a more wholesome life.

One more toot toot! (After all, it did take me five years to write this book. Besides, I most definitely consider false modesty a self-defeating cultural hang-up!) I am proud to say *Chiquita's Cocoon* has been adopted as a textbook as well as supplementary reading in junior high schools, high schools, colleges, universities and various other educational and correctional institutions across the country. *Toooot!*

I expressly wrote *Chiquita's Cocoon* for the Latina woman because I firmly believe she is in a cultural crisis. As Latina women we've yet to have our place among the stars, but I promise you, we will! Now, I'm so glad that this book is for Everywoman.

For *Chiquita's Cocoon* to have touched and improved the lives of non-Latino women, my cup runneth over! I pray we all go forward, sharing our similarities and embracing our differences. *¡Adelante, mujeres!* Go for it, ladies!

Bettina

Contents

xvii

Contents

Contents

Introduction

How This Book Was Written—and Why

This book began as a simple autobiography of my growing up Latina. I say "simple" because I planned to tell my story from a personal point of view with no research, no statistics and no quotations. It would be a straight narrative, written from my memory and the oral history of those who would help jog that memory.

I had not gone far into my life story when I realized that although I wanted to share my experiences of growing up Latina, I also needed to compare my emotions, perceptions and behavior with those of other Latinas. I was particularly concerned with those experiences which induced deep ambiguous feelings. One set of feelings told me I would grow up, get married early, have a large family and dutifully serve a husband. A conflicting set of feelings rose from a voice deep inside me and was saying *No!* to such a lifestyle and everything that went with it. I wanted much, much more. Most differently, I wanted a lifestyle in which a husband waited and doted on *me*! The conflict left me unsettled. The question of whether to live a "traditional" Latina lifestyle or an "opposing" lifestyle had always been a distressing one. My choices were to be honest with myself and go for the lifestyle I really wanted, or to live, in a sense, a whole lifetime of lies in the traditional lifestyle in which I was reared but was fiercely opposed to.

I began to wonder if other Latinas experienced similar conflicts. Was I just imagining them? If other Latinas did share similar feelings, would they admit them openly? Consequently, I found myself (casually, at first) asking other Latinas, "When you were growing up, were things like this for you?" And, "How did you feel about them?" I'd ask my sisters, "Did mamá really say things like this?" Exploring the answers to these and other questions was fun. I even thought up a new, simple book—their stories and mine combined in a light, entertaining format.

As time went on, however, and I talked to more *mujeres* ["women"] more seriously, I began to hear *other* things—the things people say when they bare their souls. Suddenly, the tide changed. The ordinary "I grew up in the barrio" stories turned into self-reproaching confessions. I was shocked. Their stories—the ones buried inside of them—were laden with problems, pressures, and oppressive cultural hang-ups! In many instances, the same cultural conflicts I had found inside myself but had managed to combat, at least partially, had devoured them completely! I found my growing-up-Latina journey much more than I had bargained for. Many times, when they cried, I cried too.

Their stories of how they *really* felt about being so culturally focused were distressing. Some women shared confessions of anger, contempt, and disgust; others, feelings of impatience and hopelessness. All were frustrated with life in general and blamed a major part of the problem on nonprogressive cultural traditions and practices, or on being Latina.

One interviewee, a prominent political figure, admitted, "Let's face it. We are what and where we are largely because of our cultural conditioning and a lot of it definitely holds us down."

An important clarification: This book does not advocate that Latinas give up their culture and tradition. While the women I interviewed did collectively say, "In being Latina there are certain parts of me that need to change," at no point did any interviewee say, "I don't want to be a Latina." We have a bountiful cultural legacy—our history, language, music, art, folklore and food—a legacy we should always treasure. The aspects of our cultural traditions that serve a useful function should be retained. Those that are harmful and self-defeating should be examined closely, their adverse effects acknowledged, then discarded. That is what this book is about.

My life and other Latinas' lives have been similar in many ways. However, we differ noticeably in outlook. Most shocking to me is how so many women's lives lack present-day ideas and solutions. I feel happy, successful and optimistic about my life, particularly about my future. My health, family and career hum in harmony. I'm free-spirited, doing what I want to do. I love every minute of life, the downs along with the ups.

In comparison, many of my Latina counterparts are not happy. They lack energy and don't seem to be living their lives with much gusto. It is painful to see them. Many are much younger than I, but their attitude is, "Well, that's the way life is; I can't do anything to change it." It seems as if they were trapped in a cocoon of some sort, needing a way out.

After discovering this outrageous imprisonment, I knew I had to write a book about it. I interviewed approximately two hundred Latinas and began to write furiously. Feeling a strong need to offer some solutions, I found myself advocating change for progress and self-actualization, yet this still wasn't enough. A vital ingredient was missing. Baking a cake without the leavening to make it rise just doesn't work. What, then, would be the basic element to make these ideas workable and help the Latina soar to new heights to a better quality of life?

As in any quest for personal change, the basic element could be none other than *courage*. Applying any self-help idea requires megadoses of personal motivation and plain, old-fashioned *courage*. *Courage* is the atom of change.

I have finally concluded that this book is not merely about the Latina's dilemmas inside her cultural cocoon. This book is mostly about *courage,* specifically the Latina's *courage*—her *courage* to face some self-truths, her *courage* to want to change, her *courage* to act differently and her *courage* to attain self-actualization.

A note to my readers:

Make this book *yours*. Communicate with it by underlining, circling and highlighting the passages that affect you, excite you or that you just want to remember.

Talk back to me in the margins. Share what you mark with friends. A marked-up book is a book well used and well read.

Bettina

PART
1

Cultural Genesis

1

Mirror, Mirror on the Wall

The white-and-black police car, the black coroner's car
and the long blue hearse filled the front yard of the old
wooden house situated at the rear of the lot. Outside,
around the short fence, neighbors stationed themselves
in small groups, looking bewildered. Inside the house,
the family gathered around a man lying, face covered, on
the double bed in the middle of the front room. The
children—Ruth, Carlos, Josephine, Jenny, Mario, Rosie,
and the one-year-old baby, Elizabeth—watched, very
still, as the English-speaking coroner asked their Spanish-speaking mother if she knew how her forty-three-
year-old husband had died. With tears rolling down her
brown yet pale-looking cheeks, she shook her head no.
The coroner looked at the children and, giving them a
tiny twinkle of hope, said, "Well, we better take a look
and see what money your father left your mom here." He

3

removed the flat, worn wallet from the dead man's pants, opened it, and pulled out two dollars. Sighing deeply, he gave the money to the mother and, shaking his head, whispered, "No English, two dollars, and seven children . . ."

CORONER'S STATUS REPORT:

Mother's Profile

Latina, age 33

7 children, ages 11, 9, 8, 7, 5, 3 and 1

No education

No English skills

No work experience

No trade skills

No familiarity with the U.S. system

Catholic

$2.00 on hand

Mother's Personality

Shy, nonconfident, fearful

The Year: 1943

The Place: United States of America

The Prognosis: This woman will submerge into her culture, which she brought with her from Mexico. She'll live a life of poverty, depression, status tension, illiteracy and sexual exploitation. She'll have a short life expectancy. Like so many of her class, she'll exist and barely survive in her cultural cocoon—void of any yen for a piece of the American dream available to her.

I was the one-year-old child. Now, nearly half a century later, I am at a Latino family gathering in Los Angeles when for no particular reason I begin to notice how the women are carrying out the party chores. Three or four are cooking, two or three are setting up tables outside and several more are preparing drinks. In the background, Latin music plays loudly and lots of children of all ages run about comfortably as though they were in their own homes. And the men? Well, the men are outside drinking beer.

The more I observe, the more I notice how little life has changed for Latinas. Here, with more than ten years of women's lib behind us, we are still stuck in traditional roles.

The Latina Dilemma: Yesterday and Today

The scenario of this party is the same as that of 1955 in my mother's house—the women working in the kitchen, the kids having fun, and the men at leisure, drinking beer.

Everyone feels in place—so to speak—except me. I feel like an outsider looking in, and I really don't know what to do with myself. I consider myself a liberated Latina, but at this party I am outnumbered and overpowered by the traditional cultural behavior of everyone else. So before I know it, I'm in the kitchen where I'm promptly provided with a full-length apron and given a work station. Unable to overcome the pressure, I silently become angry with myself because, in order to "belong," I have allowed myself to be manipulated back into the traditional role.

My preference would be to grab a beer and join the men outside. While I really consider doing this, I also weigh the consequences. Most of the women would become angry. Some might say, "She's always trying to be different." Some might remark, "What a flirt." And the insecure ones would curse under their breath, thinking, *I just know she's after my husband.* With all this running through my head, I dry my hands on the flour-sack apron and tearfully chop away at the onions.

It's maddening for me. All of us are in our late thirties and forties, college-educated, modern, liberated (or so I thought), well read, knowledgeable about current affairs and, of course, trying the latest diet. Why, then, are we all behaving so traditionally Hispanic?

Except for me, no one seems concerned with the way things are going this afternoon. After all, the voices in the kitchen are happy, the laughter from the guys outside pitches in and out, and the kids are screaming in tones that let their mothers know everything is fine.

It's getting late, and the men are complaining about being hungry. "Well," I'm about to say, "why don't you guys get in here and help," when my hostess graciously beats me with, "No problem, guys. I'll get the kids to make some snacks for you. Dinner won't be until much later."

(No problem?*%$!*&! No problem? We're knee deep in cases of chicken to be cut, a dozen heads of lettuce are rolling around the floor waiting for a shower and a swift knife, and the corn on the cob, bulging out of grocery bags, is screaming for a shave!)

"No problem," I sarcastically mimic to myself. "But now we'll need someone to supervise the kids."

Boy, was I wrong! I should have known better.

Before I know it, there are five little girls, ranging in age from five to ten, fixing he-man sandwiches. Giggling and laughing, they slap the sandwiches together as if they have been doing it all their lives. They don't even balk. The command has been given and these little girls clearly understand their roles. Skillfully and proudly they serve their creations to the men.

At that moment, I don't know whether to cry or scream, but I definitely know what's annoying me. Although I had slipped back into the traditional role for a moment, I was conscious of my decision. But these little girls have already been programmed to obey and serve men in the same way my generation was—by our mothers! The only difference was that sandwiches had replaced tacos.

Sadly I think, "Fifteen to twenty years from now these little girls will be making party food in their kitchens and their men will be outside, drinking beer."

What arouses my frustration is not the making of sandwiches or the mundane duty of serving men, but rather the inability and failure to break old habits, particularly those that are oppressive. I often fail too, when my need to belong overcomes my desire to be equal. It is through many bitter failures that I also know how hard and painful it is to look at ourselves and our lives, and to accept the fact that our lives are imperfect.

Pleasure and Pain of Learning About Ourselves

As Latinas, we have traditionally played the "let me wait on you" role with men to the *extreme,* because it's been culturally *instilled* in us. As insignificant as this may seem on the surface, it is one of the most harmful traditions for Latinas and for other women whose cultures emphasize subservience to men, because it is psychologically damaging. If that's all women are programmed to do and if that's all they ever do, everyone eventually believes that it's all they *can* do. Worse, women themselves condition men to expect to be served, thereby perpetuating an attitude of servitude at all times, just like at this party.

Having to wait on men constantly is oppressive, for it leaves a woman with little or no freedom for herself. Women caught in this programming are basically declaring to their mates, "You come first, therefore, I come last." This hardly enhances a woman's self-esteem.

Throughout the party, I make mental notes. All of us are Latinos or of Spanish-speaking races. Our backgrounds are immensely diversified: students, housewives, secretaries, mechanics, administrators, teachers, lawyers and doctors. The host and hostess are Mexican and Cuban; some couples are Mexican; others consider themselves Mexican American, Chicanos or Latinos. The media has labeled all of us Hispanic, which to me is odd because Hispanic comes from Hispana, meaning Spain, and most Spanish-speaking people in the United States are either U.S.-born or from Mexico or Central American countries. For simplicity, I use Latinas or Latinos.

I start counting the number of children per couple and I'm startled to see we're still having lots of babies. I mean, the pill has been out since the sixties and yet each couple has at least three children and most have five. One couple has seven and is considering having another. (Ave Maria Purisima!) Where were we when the pill was invented? Where was I?

I have four children. But did I ever stop to *think* of how many children I really wanted? No. Did my husband? No. Who, then, decided for us? I think in all of us there's a little Latino voice of conditioning telling us what to do, how to act and how to live. And unless we change, we will be what we are conditioned to be—by this little Latino voice.

Speaking of children, I am surprised to see Latino parents at the party still relating to their children according to sex, because I thought some influence from the women's lib movement had to have affected most parents. Putting it bluntly: Males get favorable attention; females are ignored.

A striking example of this presents itself when a little girl runs up to her mother and asks if she can get another soda. The mother instantly replies, "No, you'll get sick," then shoos the child away. Five minutes later the little girl's brother asks the mother the same thing and the mother says, "*Ay, mi hijo* ["my son"], look at you. You're hot and sweaty." Soothingly, she pushes his hair away from his forehead and says, "Are you having fun, hijo? Okay, then, go ahead and get a soda."

To me, this isn't about who gets the soda and who doesn't but rather who gets the attention, the concern, the touch of the mother's hand, the feeling of importance. Who is made to feel weak and diminished? As I thought more about this, I couldn't help but wonder what possible chance there is for a fair relationship between the sister and the brother. Latina girls rarely have a position at all. Even though they're close to their mothers, the mother is still partial to the boys. Naturally, a son pampered by his mother would, no doubt, expect the same attention from his sister and, later, his wife!

Throughout the day, I see repeated instances of Latino parents, because of cultural conditioning and habit, treating their children in the same manner in which they had been treated.

A more telling incident occurs when a little girl and a little boy trip over each other. Both children cry, but the boy cries louder. The father walks over to see what is wrong and literally steps over the little girl. Totally ignoring her, he picks up his son and carries him into the house.

I pick up the little girl and comfort her until she has composed herself. She knows and accepts the fact that no one is really concerned about her. Her programming is already in effect. It's obvious that Latino parents have culturally inherited sexual biases. Males are definitely supreme.

When the firstborn is a son, a double tragedy for Latinas occurs. The Latina loses her status to her son. Also, by giving birth to a son who will be reared like the father, the Latina will have two machos to contend with.

Even worse, because the Latina has been conditioned to believe that only a son will validate her husband's machismo, she gladly rushes to assist in the vicious cycle.

She assists by celebrating and agreeing with her husband that he is, indeed, fulfilled with the birth of his almighty son. Her thinking: "See, honey, I'm a good wife. I gave you a son to show off to your friends, to make you feel manly, to carry on your name. He is so special to you that I'll treat him special."

When the firstborn is a girl, there is nearly always a feeling of disappointment, felt particularly by the father. He sees her as a burdensome responsibility, someone he'll have to someday marry off. The wife feels guilty and diminished, knowing she did not fulfill her husband's expectations. Her relatives and *comadres* ["female friends"], however, soothe her by reminding her, *"Qué bueno que tuviste una niña primero para que ella te ayude con los demás niños"* ["It's good your firstborn is a girl. She'll be able to help you with the other children you will have"]. This kind of statement underscores the fact that Latinas are looked upon more as utilitarian objects than as persons!

From birth the Latina child is held in low esteem. As long as Latinas and their female offspring remain agreeable victims of this oppression, they will continue to suffer from low self-esteem. Unless this chain of self-crucifying conditioning is broken, it will remain a vicious cycle affecting generation after generation.

It is crucial for Latinas to become aware of their role in this cycle so that they can begin to oppose and change it. It can only be broken when Latinas end their complicity in this cultural castration and say *¡basta!* ["enough"]. They must develop their own self-respect and instill self-respect in their children, both female and male.

Inside Chiquita's Cocoon

Any Latina who is living or has lived any part of her life like the women at the party exists in a cultural cocoon perpetuated through outdated traditions and practices. It is a homespun cocoon that on the surface appears cozy, but that in reality is smothering her in a living death. It's an unquestioned, unchallenged cocoon that in the mightiest era of women's lib ever, continues to impede the Latina's full development and sacrifices her God-given human potential! Too many of the customs and practices inside Chiquita's cocoon are unhealthy, have negative effects and result in self-defeating behavior.

The party story is merely an overview of the Latina dilemma. The rest of Part I addresses the critical issues: poverty, machismo manipulation, excessive maternal guilt, religious persecution, lack of education and lack of goal-setting and life-planning skills. For some readers, the discussion of these sensitive culture-related issues may be difficult to accept—exposés usually are. Although we know certain truths to be factual, reading about them makes them more visible, threatening and undeniable. We may even see ourselves, a friend, a relative or a loved one in these chapters.

Those who feel threatened should put their fears aside and think of the courageous Latinas who bared their feelings in this book (as one of them said, her "lesser self") just to help others avoid making the same mistakes. From them, I heard all the anguish, pain and cries for help I ever want to hear as they willingly recounted their cultural-related shortcomings. It was as if they were relieved that at last someone who understood them was willing to listen. For many, the dominant emotions of insecurity, resentment, loneliness and fear left very little room for the emotions of joy, happiness and self-love. So put your nervousness and fears aside. You are not alone.

Facing Up

We *must* deal with all this devitalizing, draining anguish once and for all. One way is to face up to what's being said in this book. You certainly don't have to agree with everything, but please accept this: Everything starts with *awareness* and every change that follows flows from that *awareness*. It behooves you to read the *entire* book, for the ultimate benefit lies in understanding the total picture and using your newly gained awareness as a stepping-stone in life.

In Part II are some suggestions and philosophies for change; that is, how to drop the old and start with the new. This section offers you some fresh ways of thinking, incentives for a winning attitude, and much, much inspiration to help you progress and attain whatever you want out of life. As in all learning, however, this section requires some study.

In our four-hundred-year history a self-help book such as this one is a rarity. Befriend this book as your unfailing companion. Carry it; use it wherever you are. I passionately believe that *Chiquita's Cocoon* has something for *everyone* and that *everyone* in *Chiquita's Cocoon* is addressing an important, much overdue need. I hope you do too.

¡Adelante!

Facts, Myths and Mitotes*

The Status of Latinas, 1983, Los Angeles Times

Population:

Of the 7,328,842 Latinas nationwide, nearly 4.3 million are of Mexican descent and have an average age of 22.

Job Status:

Most Latinas remain in low-paying jobs as factory workers or typists. Latinas earn 49 cents for every dollar a white male earns. White women earn 58 cents and black women 54 cents.

*Gossip.

Education:

On the average, Latinas have completed 8.8 years of school compared to 12.4 for the general population.

Single Parents:

Women head about 20 percent of all Latino families. The number of poor Latinas doubled between 1972 and 1981, from about 800,000 to 1.6 million. Of those households headed by a Latina with children under 18, 65 percent were under poverty level.

Divorce:

The divorce rate for Latinas rose from 81 to 146 divorced persons per 1,000 in active marriages between 1970 and 1981. (The comparable 1981 rate was 118 for white women and 289 for black women.)

Activism:

"Latinas have a history of strength and activism," says Adelaida del Castillo of UCLA, "including a record of strikes spanning almost every area of their labor from fields to factories." In the last decade, Latinas have taken a more active role in education as parent council members, teachers' aides and school officials. Latinas are also active on a variety of fronts, through unions, networks, higher education, law, business, social agencies and community groups.

Future:

> Maria Rodriguez, an attorney for the Mexican American Legal Defense and Educational Fund, says, "I'm very optimistic about the future because I continue to meet outstanding Latinas with some real leadership ability and concern about Latinas as women. *Latinas have unique problems* that we need to address if we want to improve conditions for all Latinos in this country."

Statistics are another way of looking at ourselves as a group. Statistics are hard to argue with. They expose gaps, provide comparisons and spell out the facts. In this set of statistics, we plainly see that Latinas are suffering economically, educationally and socially.

In 1974, the situation was even worse. The U.S. Department of Labor reported that women of Spanish origin (this particular study included Puerto Ricans, Cubans and Mexicans) had a median income of $3,065.

What? $3,065?

When I ran into this statistic, I really became alarmed. How could this be? No one could live on $3,065 per year, not even in 1974! That year I was working at a university as an administrator; I was earning $15,000! Why had I assumed all other Latinas were doing about the same? Of all the statistics on Latinas, this figure of $3,065 riled me the most. It was a hard fact for me to swallow, to believe and to face. Now here we are in the nineties and on the whole Latinas remain an impoverished, suffering class. Something is wrong! Why the abject poverty? Why haven't Latinas progressed? Intellectually we're no different from anyone else. What is the problem?

The Stumbling Blocks of Ethnic Erroneous Zones

Perhaps what we need to do, in addition to digesting these painful statistics, is to explore our lives from a deeper, more personal perspective. We should take an honest look at ourselves from *within,* examining how we think, talk and act. The Latinas in this book have done this, and I believe there is much we can learn from them. While their stories interwoven with mine by no means constitute a sociological study, one theme surfaced over and over: We Latinas are who and where we are largely because of our cultural conditioning, much of which holds us down. Almost everyone expressed this point of view. Because the concerns were many and of a grievous nature, they fill this chapter as well as the next one.

Here goes. *Courage, Chiquita!*

The most common negative cultural influences are:

- Accepting poverty and denying the importance of money.
- Validating racism.
- Being overly ethnocentric and fearful of challenging the traditional role.
- The fear of denying our heritage.
- A reluctance to become Anglicized.
- A resistance to biculturalism.
- A lack of education and personal goals.

17

Add to these a myriad of misdirected attitudes toward materialism, machismo and religion and you may begin to recognize some of the ethnic erroneous zones that stifle our progress. For definition, erroneous zones are self-defeating behaviors we are caught up in and that hold us back. We all have erroneous zones. Equally so, we all have the power to free ourselves by facing them, understanding their roots and effects and moving on to more wholesome living.

Poverty First and foremost is the subject of money. Why? Money is one of our greatest needs. Unfortunately my interviews told me many Latinas think otherwise.

Money is considered by Latinas to be almost sinful. "Money," Latinas say, "causes problems." "Money," they declare, "isn't necessary for happiness." "Money," my interviewees told me, "isn't important."

What? Money *not* important? Money is *very* important! Money buys food, housing, health, education, justice and travel. Money provides security, stability, peace of mind, self-confidence and inner happiness. As long as we live in a money-oriented system, money has to be one of the most important items in our lives because it gives us the means with which to take care of ourselves and those who depend on us.

Feeling guilty about enjoying money or having it or wishing you had more comes from erroneous spiritual and cultural attitudes. For Catholic Latinas, the Catholic Church would have us believe that poverty is a virtue, when in reality it is a trap.

"Happy are the poor" is nothing more than a slogan used to deceive people, to keep them under control and from reaching out for more. Look, for example, at the poor people in Mexico who do their traditional pilgrimages to the basilica on their knees. They ask God for more abundance in their lives, but most likely they are asking for jobs so they can feed their families. Although this pilgrimage is religiously respected, the reality is you can't get a job while on your knees for hours at a time. You get a job by putting in applications or by creating your own livelihood!

The Catholic Church is not poor. Many of its parishioners are, however—particularly Hispanics around the world. The Catholic Church could teach prosperity as well as it could teach acceptance of poverty, but it chooses not to. Have you ever wondered why? Latinas are poor because they've been religiously and culturally conditioned to accept poverty as an immutable fact! (Obviously, if the church says poverty is good for us, then it must be so.)

I can no longer believe this. We need prosperity in our lives. We need prosperity lectures and indoctrination. If you are Latina and Catholic, it is probable that you've never heard of prosperity lectures, right? Well, you should get interested because at a prosperity lecture you learn how to make more money. Prosperity lectures are often sponsored by a bank, your community college, local businesses or even television. They can be general as in "Think and Grow Rich" or related to a specific area, as in "How to Get Rich in Real Estate," "How to Double Your Savings" or "How to Exceed Your Salary Potential." Check your newspaper for such events and sign up. Remember, feeling guilty about money is phony, unrealistic and self-defeating.

I love money! I am very bold about it. With money I feed my children, provide for their health needs, educate them and get them out of trouble. I can run my car, make the house payments and take a vacation with my husband. Without money life is pretty dull: no books, magazines or videos, no lunches, no clothes, no cosmetics or nice perfumes, no conferences, no traveling, no entertainment and no future plans. When I'm broke I feel ill and depressed, spiritless and stuck.

I grew up with the disease of poverty. At the age of twelve, no longer able to stand my daily potatoes and beans diet, sick of boring, uneventful living, weary of seeing my mother worrying over our next meal, impatient for a better life—I left home!

Let's be truthful. To be without money is to suffer. No one says it better than Unity Minister Catherine C. Ponders in *The Dynamic Laws of Prosperity,* "Poverty fills prisons with thieves and murderers. Poverty drives men and women to the vices of alcohol, drugs, prostitution and even suicide. It drives potentially fine, talented children to delinquency and crime. It causes worry, strain and tension, which lead to poor physical and mental health. To live in poverty is to live in a depressed state, a bona fide sickness often undetected and accepted as a normal way to live."

The American Heart Association in an article called "Poverty Kills" states that the poor are more likely than others to develop heart disease. In fact, they found that "poor males as a group, regardless of race, are almost 40% more likely to die of heart disease than wealthier males. Among women, the rate was 27% higher when comparing the poor to the more affluent."

Poverty, not money, is the real sin!

Racism   Racism is a sensitive, complex and worldwide problem. Racism, however, is *not* the *sole* cause of our woes, as many Latinas believe. Racism is just one of the many negative hang-ups that we've allowed to dominate our thinking, stopping us from succeeding.

True Confessions of Latinas
Who Want out of Their Cocoons

Ethnocentrism   Many Latinas are fiercely ethnocentric. Whether we want to face this or not, it needs to be said. We tend to remain immersed in our culture, failing to reach out for anything but the familiar. Why? Because we feel protected and safe in our cultural cocoon. We're afraid to venture out. Of course, it's easier to stay within our familiar traditions of culture, near those who believe as we do, who accept us as we are and who we feel are the only ones from whom we can receive love. What we should realize is that often this very attachment holds us back and even hurts us. Christina, twenty-two, writes:

> I grew up and lived in the barrio all my life and whenever
> I wanted to do anything outside the barrio, my friends
> and family questioned my motives like you wouldn't
> believe. What for? You want to be white? Don't you like
> being brown? *¿Qué más quieres?* ["What more do you
> want?"] Now, I look back and I can see how emotionally
> and mentally confining my friends and family were. The
> more I tried to reach out for something more or differ-
> ent, the more pressure was placed on me to stay put.

Latina "groupies" hold on to each other through peer group pressure. They believe that socializing with "others" (non-Latinos) is a no-no. Even thinking of trying to be like others is close to treason. Afraid, but not really knowing why, they restrict themselves to their environmental cocoon. For the most part, Latinas will go only to those events where they are sure they will be with their own kind.

The irony is that groupies are groupies out of habit and custom, not because they individually have identified any logical reason they shouldn't socialize with others. Jenny, who attends a small college in a small town, geared herself to get to know a lot of new people on campus. She told me:

> My being Latina was no problem for the new people I met, but it seemed a big issue for the Latinas who didn't feel like I did. Regardless, I joined clubs and got involved in a lot of activities, and in most instances I was almost always the only Latina member. Occasionally, I'd invite my Latina friends to various functions, but I always got no for an answer. Personally, I feel it was good for me to get involved. I'm in college to expand and broaden my thinking and to learn what makes others tick. If I limit myself to a single group, I'm limiting myself, period.

Being overly ethnocentric and accepting the traditional ways cost forty-six-year-old Alicia years of suffering, and almost her life. She reported:

> I was born in Mexico and came to the United States when I was thirteen. I suffered as a battered wife through two early marriages while my family and friends looked on. I was taught and told over and over again not to discuss my personal problems with anyone and to bear my cross like a good wife. Instead of helping me, my family reinforced my burden.

Latinas fear standing up to family and friends for things they believe in or need. This fear comes from early childhood training and lack of status within the family unit. It is, therefore, understandable that the Latina is fearful of challenging her traditional role. But it is worse—limiting and unhealthy—to permit herself to be mentally and physically abused.

Denying Our Heritage   The fear that Latinas will deny their heritage if they leave home is a myth. If you want to be a Latina, Chicana, Mexican or Hispana, you can be one anywhere. Leaving home has very little to do with denying one's heritage and much to do with emotional blackmail. How many times have we heard, "If you leave home you can never be a good Latina again." Or *"si fueras una hija buena, no me harías esto"* ["if you were a good and loving daughter, you wouldn't do this to me"]. Parents who place this guilt trip on their offspring, young or adult, are self-serving. It's understandable to hold on to your offspring when the need is acute, as in the care of the elderly or sick. But when it is not, parents need to recognize that they can make their offspring dependent and weak. If they would consider their children's future, they would realize how much they hinder them.

It's heartbreaking to hear Latinas say, "I don't want my children moving away when they grow up." This attitude only discourages the young from venturing out to experience life independently. Furthermore, statements like "I don't want my kids going away to college" are equally upsetting, because attending college away from home affords one of the best opportunities for personal growth.

When a Latina breaks away from the home roost, she's labeled a loose woman rather than someone seeking independence and space in which to grow. Isabel, for example, left home at twenty and now she says:

> In my early twenties, I was labeled such a woman. I left home after I found my first job and for about ten years I floated around from job to job. I was looking for something I could really sink my teeth into. Of course, I would go home to visit and always there would be the inference of, "Still messing around, Isabel? Can't you get satisfied and settle down?" My father always preached how *la familia es lo más importante* ["the family is all-important"], but once I stepped outside that boundary I was *nada* ["nothing"]. You know what I think? We just haven't learned to love by letting go.

It is true that leaving home is one of the most difficult things to do, since Latinas typically have lived in barrio blocks generation after generation. The cultural cocoon can swallow up people almost totally, leaving them barely able to function outside that cocoon.

The move my husband and I made from Fresno, California, to Los Angeles, a 180-miles-one-way jaunt, with three young children, was horribly traumatic. Neither of us had ever left our hometown. When we reached Los Angeles all we could think of was getting back to Fresno. Imagine! Two adults unable to adjust. Our emotional ties with our families were so strong that we spent every weekend for four years going home! In every way—psychologically, physically, emotionally and financially—our early conditioning cost us dearly.

While living and dying on the same barrio block is cozy, and probably meets someone *else's* need, it is also like being stranded on an island where no outside influences or experiences can reach you. Even those who manage to leave as adults, like my husband and I did, find themselves hurting, ill prepared and lost.

Latinas who limit themselves to their barrio blocks are denying themselves life's vast opportunities. Barrio blocks inside cultural cocoons reinforce the same values over and over, leaving little room for learning or change, both of which are necessary for progress.

It's essential for Latinas to live their *own* lives upon reaching adulthood. Sure, you might feel like you are severing your past and your roots, but if you feel strong about them, they will be a part of you wherever you go. Growing up, leaving home and remaining Latina *can* go hand in hand.

Fear of Anglos   Fear of Anglos (and of being Anglicized) is another phobia Latinas acquire from cultural upbringing. I know I did. Latinas without skills and education are especially intimidated by Anglos and others who make them feel inferior and threatened.

I was just four years old when I was first intimidated by an Anglo woman. She was our welfare worker and came to our home to check up on us on a monthly basis. For some reason, she always sat and my mother and I stood together in the center of the room facing her. I will never forget it! I would cling to my mother's leg, sensing her nervousness and fear. The Anglo woman always had a barrage of questions (in English, of course), which she shot at my mother like piercing arrows. Having no English skills, feeling intimidated and threatened, my mother could say very little and was forced to listen to verbal abuse. Do you know why *I* at four years of age also felt intimidated and scared? I was copying my mother's behavior. I wanted my mother to fight back, but she couldn't.

Fear is an overwhelming emotion. When you're scared it's

hard to pull yourself together, let alone handle matters or people. When you fear the unknown (in this case, non-Latinos) it's even worse because your feelings of inferiority restrict you from acting on your own behalf. Panic sets in, anger rises and, without an outlet, festers into contempt and hate. Soon you're saying, "I hate them" or "I can't stand them." You rationalize defensively, "I never want to be like an Anglo." Eventually these emotions build up. You harbor long-standing feelings and become phobic in your dealings with Anglos, which results in self-defeating attitudes. My mother, like millions of other Latinas, avoided and feared the vast unknown of communicating in other than her own language.

So think for a minute. Is the Anglo really the enemy? Or is the enemy our fear of the unknown and our reluctance to conquer it? Yes, Anglos, or anyone else for that matter, can intimidate you, make you feel inferior and threaten you, but only when they are more knowledgeable than you and only when you let them.

Earlier I said I would never forget the intimidating scenarios of my childhood. I have not and I've sworn that no one would ever again intimidate me. I promised myself that no one would ever talk to me like that and get away with it. I vowed to learn English and practice my written and verbal skills until I could express myself as well as any Anglo in any situation. There was a reason I majored in English and communications and was a tough debater in college. I wanted to play the game and *win*. Latinas have to learn the rules and be willing to put themselves on the scrimmage line.

Latinas who have been nurtured by the Latino culture are not necessarily going to become Anglicized by exposing themselves to the Anglo world. If you want to be a Latina, Chicana, Mexican or Hispana, you can be one anywhere and with anyone. Remember this, and let's move forward.

Having the Choice of Who to Be

Being bilingual and bicultural is an asset. It is having *twice* as much as most folks. How fortunate can Latinas be? Aurora, who was educated partially in Mexico and partially in California, puts it nicely:

> My best asset is being bilingual and bicultural and being both Mexican and American. I'm comfortable and secure in *pachangas* ["cultural parties"] with close friends and relatives. I'm also secure when I'm involved with my many other friends. I have the best of both worlds.

Latinas can have the best of both worlds as well as a choice of who to be. Elisa A. Martinez, fifty-one, an elementary teacher of severely handicapped children and the former director of Teatro de los Pobres, lives on the Juarez border. She says, "I'm glad my mother crossed *that* river. There's so much more here." A mother of six (five with college degrees), she wrote:

Having the Choice of Who to Be
Elisa A. Martinez

> As Mexican Americans, we are often criticized for not flowing in the mainstream of America. Why do "they" insist on speaking "that language" and retaining "that" culture when "they" live in the United States?

I can't answer that question for anyone else.
But as for me, I find it makes life more
interesting.

By all appearances, I am one person but in reality
I am two.

It is one of me who cries when she hears melancholy
memories of mother and father; it is the other who
sighs when she hears "Goodnight Sweetheart," with
her memories of friends, proms and malts at the drive-
in.

It is one of me who enjoys a slice of medium rare
roast beef and the other who wraps it in a tortilla
and downs it with hot chili sauce.

It is one of me who jerks in rhythm to "Billie Jean"
and the other who swirls gaily to corridos[1] and steps
in rhythm to a cumbia.[2]

It is one of me who prepares for Santa Claus and the
other who breaks the piñata at the Posada.[3]

It is one of me who wants to be always on time and
the other who gets there just a little bit late.

It is one of me who interprets Serafina in Tennessee
Williams' "Rose Tattoo" and the other who becomes

1. A Mexican polka.
2. A salsa-type dance.
3. A twelve-day Christmas celebration.

"La Siempreviva" in Luis Basurto's "Cada Quién Su Vida."[4]

It is one of me who carves out the face in the pumpkin for Halloween and the other who cleans the sepulcro[5] on Día de Los Muertos.[6]

It is one of me who buys the smoke alarm for the safety of the family and the other who has it disconnected when it drives us mad every time a tortilla burns.

It is one of me who buys medication at the drugstore and the other who washes it down with estafiate.[7]

It is one of me who can appreciate Beverly Sills in concert and the other me who can appreciate "The Poet and Peasant Overture" played beautifully by a group of mariachis.[8]

It is one of me who takes great pains to speak English correctly, giving great care to the rules of grammar, and the other *me* who says Qué cute![9] and Simón que yes![10]

It is one of me who celebrates Mother's Day on the second Sunday in May and the other *me* who celebrates again on May 10.

4. La Siempreviva is the leading lady in "Cada Quién Su Vida" ["To Each His Own"].
5. A grave.
6. Day of the Dead.
7. A Mexican tea used for health purposes.
8. A group of musicians.
9. How cute!
10. Of course!

It is one of me who feels the patriotic emotion
when the Stars and Stripes go by and the other who
elates at the tri-colored flag with the eagle in the
center as she marches by to the rhythm of the bugles.

The other day as I was cleaning the house, I was
singing that popular Nelson/Iglesias release "To All
the Girls I Loved Before." My husband, who
incidentally does not appreciate my singing (another
Mexican custom), asked, "And who are you, Willie or
Julio?"

How neat, I thought, that I DO have a choice.

More Facts, Myths and Mitotes

Education: Our Biggest Stumbling Block

Lack of education is the most obvious and most serious hang-up for Latinas. *Intercambio Femeniles,* a national Latina newsletter from Berkeley, California, reported in 1982 that only 44 percent of Latinas who are twenty-five years and older have a high school diploma and a mere 6 percent have completed four or more years of college. In California, where 2.24 million Latinas live, Latinas have a 50 percent high school dropout rate. Poverty, early pregnancy, marriage and the desire to enter the work force are the sources of this problem, according to statisticians.

Why Latinas Resist Education

Many say it's the lack of role models that makes education seem unimportant to Latinas. This is certainly true, but then the argument goes right back to, "Why aren't there any?" There aren't enough role models because too few Latinas attempt higher education. Of those who do, only a small percentage make it through a four-year college.

Latinas are barely making it through high school. If they can't get through high school, how are they going to make it *to* college? *In* college? More important, at what point of their lives do Latinas begin to reject education, and why? Is it when the kindergarten teacher tells them they may only speak English at school? Or in fourth grade, when the easy ABC's turn into the more difficult social sciences? Or in junior high, where taking group showers is a requirement? Or maybe in high school, where the temptations of sex, romance and marriage are dominant, as is the need to have clothes, a car and a job with which to buy them?

So what? These and other seemingly insurmountable problems have to be overcome. Other groups go through the same experiences and they manage to make it. Overcoming the unpleasantness of any situation is the mark of a strong person. Getting an education is not a party. College is not a dream. It's a challenge. It's years of demanding courses, tough competition, serious studying and financial stress. Sticking it out four years or more takes a lot of *courage*.

Perhaps Latinas reject education because of their conditioning during their formative years. They are expected to carry heavy loads of work at home. Those who also have to do farm work are even more drained of energy. Weary, they carry negative attitudes to school and cannot achieve as they should. With these motivation killers and lack of familial encouragement, Latinas have to go it alone—a Herculean task.

Nevertheless, Latinas must realize that if they are going to make it on the educational scene they will have to be strong, dare to be different and ignore their environmental barriers. Maria, once a leader on her barrio block and now an attorney in Denver, remembers how she was treated when she went home during semester breaks:

> My friends and family shunned me and treated me as though I didn't belong anymore.

Irene of Texas says:

> When I came home with my Ph.D., no one was impressed. My family's attitude was "So what?" And my mother asked why I was still chasing rainbows.

Education is a serious task. From preschool on, every Latino child needs support and motivation to achieve. Latino parents must offer this support and motivation. They must share the education process from day one, so their children can excel in school. Yes, it's emotionally and psychologically difficult to get involved in anything when you don't know where your next meal is coming from. Nonetheless, education is the solution to cyclical poverty and Latinas in particular need to concentrate on the solution, not the problem!

We can start by realizing, really realizing, the monumental importance of education by drawing on and using inner strength, by adopting "I'm going to stick to it" attitudes and by setting some self-imposed goals and standards of achievement.

I wanted to quit school when I was in kindergarten because the teacher told me I couldn't speak Spanish in school. "But," I

argued, "Spanish is all I know." She told me not to talk unless I
spoke English and moved me to the back of the room. I went home
and solemnly announced I was quitting school. My family laughed,
saying the police would come after me. As soon as I heard the word
police I had images of jail, and I knew I would never get to play on
the school merry-go-round again. So I went back, concluding that
even if I couldn't speak Spanish, I could still play on the merry-go-
round.

Six months later, after the novelty of the merry-go-round wore
off, I went home and said again, "School is boring. I'm quitting."
The family laughed again, then added, "Either stay in school or go
to work in the fields with your uncle." Well, even as a six-year-old
I knew the difference between a fourteen-hour backbreaking
field-work day and a four-hour patty-cake shift at school. Back to
school I went.

Naturally I was bored. I was stubbornly sitting in the back of
the classroom, refusing to participate. I really *could* speak English.
I just preferred to speak Spanish because it felt natural and warm.
And, besides, why should I speak English just because the teacher
said I had to?

Finally one day, tired of the boredom and the merry-go-
round, I suddenly unleashed all the English I had held back for
months and became a functional kindergartner. Still, I have never
forgiven the school system for stealing from me the fluency of my
spoken Spanish. If I could sue them for this infringement, I would.

Suppose that my family had accepted my childish decision to
quit school and sent me to work in the fields? It could have easily
happened. It too often does in our culture. I wholeheartedly thank
my family for *making* me stay in school.

United States Secretary of Education Lauro F. Cavazos, the

first Hispanic cabinet member in our nation's history, says, "What
Hispanic and all other children need today are parents and teachers
who care. Education must begin at home." Later in a subsequent
statement appearing in *The Fresno Bee* he said, "Hispanic parents
deserve much of the blame for the high dropout rate among their
children and this could have dire consequences for the U.S. econ-
omy."

His statement is validated by the courageous Latina Rosita,
who for years worked as a school attendance clerk:

> I know for a fact that Hispanic parents don't try hard
> enough to keep their kids in school. I call them and call
> them to send their kids to school, but they don't. They
> say they have too many problems. Hispanic student ab-
> sences are an epidemic. Boy, when I was raising my five
> kids we had problems too, but I sent them to school no
> matter what. No matter if my husband came home
> drunk and raised hell all night; no matter if he beat me;
> no matter if there was no food in the house; no matter
> if the bills were unpaid—no matter what the problem
> was, I sent my kids to school every day.

What it all really means is that:

> You forfeit your chance for life at its fullest when you
> withhold your best effort in learning. When you give only
> the minimum to learning, you receive only the minimum
> in return. Even with your parents' best example and
> your teachers' best efforts, in the end it is your work that
> determines how much and how well you learn. When

you work to your full capacity, you can hope to attain the knowledge and skills that will enable you to create your future and control your destiny. If you do not, you will have your future thrust upon you by others. Take hold of your life, apply your gifts and talents, work with dedication and self-discipline. Have high expectations for yourself and convert every challenge into an opportunity.

—From *A Nation at Risk* by the National Commission on Excellence in Education, U.S. Department of Education

The Hispanic Dream

We've all heard the words "the American Dream" over and over, but what exactly is it? The American Dream begins with an education and ends with a good-paying job. Educating oneself and working means money, a home, a car, vacations, entertainment, health care and a secure retirement. The Hispanic Dream should be the same.

Education has many rewards, the best being the earning power it can yield. A startling statistic: By the year 2065, the average salary will be $176,000 per year! Can you imagine your children earning that kind of money? Will they have the education they need to earn that basic salary and the skills with which to compete? We'd better see to it that they do or they'll be poor.

For now, however, you, as a mujer, can get *your* education and the earning power that goes with it. Never before in America's history have the opportunities for women been so fantastic! There are more women than men in college today and the same will be true in the future. The majority of workers are women. Whether married or single, women are taking responsibility for their own financial support. Women are buying their own cars, houses, furnishings and obtaining credit cards. An incredible number of businesses are being opened and successfully operated by women everywhere.

Another enticing phenomenon to consider is the fact that the New Age wave (living longer and healthier lives) means you can pursue more than just one career in your lifetime. Already many men and women are experiencing three or four major career changes. You can start or change careers at almost any age. If you married young and had children early, for example, chances are you will be through raising your family by age forty. If you live to be at least seventy, you will have many years to fill with something meaningful.

Believe me, there is nothing like education to give you position and power. Knowledge *is* power. For instance, take this one little piece of indisputable information that is taught from fourth grade on: *The male sperm determines the sex of the infant.* Why do I bring this particular fact up? Because for centuries women have been degraded, divorced, dethroned, exiled, tortured and put to death for giving birth to females. For centuries, and even today, men (particularly machos) blame women for not producing sons, when it is *they* who are the ones with the empty shooter! I often think of the tremendous empowerment women would have gained had they only known this fact sooner. It's time for women, mothers and daughters alike, to use this powerful wisdom to stop taking the blame and put it where it truly belongs.

What does all this prove? It proves women can make it. They don't have to settle for early marriage, large families and dependency on men. The opportunity for the Hispanic Dream to come true is real.

It is real at least for brave new women.

Cultural Barriers to Goal Setting and Life Planning

Goal setting. These are important, important words. Goal setting is not a term one hears very often within the Latino culture. I first heard it while working at the university and the concept baffled me because the words themselves had no meaning for me. When colleagues at the university asked me what my goals were, I would naïvely respond, "I really don't have any." My colleagues looked at me as if to say, "Look, you dummy, everybody has goals!" After all, I was twenty-eight years old.

What I quickly found out was that, yes, practically *everyone* at the university had definite goals and life plans. I, however, had come from a small town to the big "U" to work while my husband went to law school. I wasn't there for myself.

Now I realize that my getting a job was a goal, as was my husband's idea of going to law school. The point is, neither one of us thought of our ideas as goals, nor had we given any real thought as to how we were going to achieve them. One day he said, "I want to go to law school in L.A." I said, "Fine. I'll get a job there while you study." Before we knew it, we were in Los Angeles.

I have searched my mind thoroughly. Surely I must have heard about the goal-setting concept somewhere. At home? Grammar school? Junior high? High school? But no, I don't recall ever having heard it. The more I thought about goal setting, life planning and status, the more I was convinced that I had never heard those words in my youth. If I had, they certainly didn't register as important, perhaps because I thought they couldn't apply to me. Even as an adult, I had problems accepting the concept. During a goal-setting exercise at a personal growth seminar I was asked where and how I saw myself in five years. My immediate reaction was, "How absurd. Nobody knows what or where they will be in five years."

I was never taught to look or plan ahead. As a child, whenever I asked my mother if we were going to do something on such-and-such a date, she would invariably respond, *"Si Dios quiere"* ["If God wills it"]. Our family rarely planned anything in advance. It was always "Let's wait and see," "*If* we have enough money," "*If* the weather holds," and, of course, the eleventh commandment, *"If God wills it."*

About the only planning we ever did was for holiday cooking—how many chickens we'd have to catch, kill, prepare and cook to make chicken and *mole* (red chile sauce); how many pounds of potatoes to peel for potato salad; how many kegs of beer to order. I suppose I remember this so well because, being the youngest, I had to catch the chickens. The rationale was, I guess, that I was closest to the ground. My oldest sister had to wring their necks and chop off their heads with an ax. The task of plucking and gutting the awful-smelling dead chickens was shared by all five girls.

Short-range goals like holiday planning, celebrating religious occasions and getting ready for school in September were easy to attain. Somehow it never occurred to us to apply the planning techniques to long-range goals, such as a better future.

I did have one thing in my favor, however, and that was my constant dreams of bigger and better things, for a life of status, financial security and happiness. Where I got those notions I really don't know. I just knew life was supposed to be exciting and fulfilling. I recall nearly driving my poor mother crazy by asking for what she labeled the impossible—a storybook, roller skates, a jack-in-the-box. Whenever I asked for just one of these she'd say, "You ask for too much. You should have been born a queen; then you could demand everything you want." Well, I never got any of the goodies, but the queen title sounded appealing.

Dreaming was my goal setting, life planning and pursuit of status. Had I had the life-planning techniques to go along with my dreams, this book would have been written a long time ago.

Now I know that goal setting and life planning are learned skills that make a vast difference in one's life. These skills give us control over our lives, make things happen instead of leaving them to chance, shape our desires and bring them into reality.

Latinas must learn life-planning skills or they will be treading water all their lives. Life will pass them by as it already has many. "I thought of doing this and that" was the response from many of my Latina interviewees, "but I could never get going in a set direction." Others said sadly, "I wish now I had something for myself. With the kids growing up so fast, I can see a lot of empty time on my hands." Yet others who really needed to let it all out cried bitter self-pitying tears saying, "I'm tired of being poor, fat and ugly. I want something for myself. But even when I think about it, I still don't know what it is I want or how to get it. Sometimes I think it's too late anyway."

Status Is Your Right

Status is definitely something Latinas need to pursue in *all* areas of their lives, from how they live and what kinds of jobs they hold to how much they make and how they perceive themselves. Why? Because status is important to self-esteem. When you have status you are proud of who you are, what you do, what you own and even with whom you socialize. The result is a good inner feeling about yourself. There is absolutely nothing wrong with being proud of yourself and your accomplishments, as long as you don't fall into an egomania trap!

Having status means enjoying a good standard of living and having others recognize your skills and merits. All of us should relish the joy of status. It makes us feel worthy and tells the world, "I'm living to my fullest potential."

Por favor, mujeres. Status means recognition and having a sense of accomplishment. Accomplishment comes from within; recognition from outside ourselves. To hunger for recognition of our worth is natural. The need is as natural as the universal need for food, shelter, love and belonging and has absolutely nothing to do with being an attention getter. Understanding the importance of all these human needs helps us live a better life. In spite of what many Latinas think, status is not synonymous with snobbery. Thinking so makes the pursuit of status seem wrong. This negative attitude is self-defeating. For example, a Latina wishes to purchase a fancy living-room set. She has the money. She has found the set she wants and loves, but she doesn't buy it because she knows its "fanciness" will bring raised eyebrows from family and friends. Since her own attitude toward status is impaired, she forgets the set

41

she loves and settles for a more conservative set. She has defeated her very own goals.

There is a distinction between having things because you really want and need them and having them only because you want to impress others. Somewhere along the way, in our cocoon, we've been persuaded that to want nice houses in good neighborhoods, new cars, money and things in general is a sin. While the Catholic Church has played a big role in keeping us "humble and poor" as well as "happy and meek," our own *gente,* the people around us, also criticize those of us who aspire to the better things in life. We who daringly enjoy material achievements are chastised with "Trying to be Anglo?" But just because you enjoy a measure of material success doesn't mean you have to feel that you've sold out!

What is so holy or so Chicano about living in overcrowded conditions or in perpetual poverty? Does the Latina really want to live all her life in substandard housing in run-down neighborhoods where crime, vandalism and gangs are rampant? Who says Latinas don't desire or deserve adequate and attractive housing with modern, luxurious conveniences? Why should Latinas allow institutions or their own culture to squelch their aspirations, to dictate their needs, to upset their vision of how *they* want to live? Why shouldn't Latinas be as comfortable as Anglo women?

My own experience reflects these inbred attitudes about material things. It was not easy shedding them. When my husband and I were dating I told him I wanted a four-bedroom, three-bath house and he responded, "That's crazy. Nobody has a four-bedroom, three-bath house." Humoring me, he added, "Besides, we'd get lost in it." Whatever possessed me to ask for such a mansion? Whatever made him think that such a house was unattainable?

Even in little ways my attitude was that I didn't deserve nice things. For years my husband told me that what I didn't have I didn't need, and I believed him. Almost all our household necessities came from garage sales and other secondhand sources. (I was well equipped too. My old Ford wagon had a bumper sticker that read: THIS CAR STOPS AT ALL GARAGE SALES.) When I would tell my husband I wanted something new and nice he would start his cultural propaganda. "You've lived without it this long, so what's the problem?" It wasn't until years later that I got the *courage* to say to him, "I know I don't absolutely need it and I know I can live without it. But, darn it, I still want it and I'm going to buy it." And finally, I did.

Driving old run-down ugly cars supports our nonmaterialistic beliefs. It's bad enough that old cars do very little for one's self-esteem, but there's an even more important issue here. Old cars are unsafe! A study in Colorado showed that fatal car accidents are a major cause of death among Latinos and that the use of old automobiles is a key factor. If we can overcome our stubbornness about buying new cars, maybe some of us will live a little longer. Why do we insist on fixing up the old "cucarachas" over and over again? As my husband would say, "Because it's cheaper to fix them than to buy new ones." What about the cost of death? I'm ashamed to write about the old heaps I've driven in my lifetime. Like my husband, it was difficult to change my thinking and get a nice-looking, safely functioning car. After all, the pieces of junk I drove were acceptable to family and peers. Everyone drove jalopies. Driving a spanking new car would have meant being "different," and, even worse, materialistic.

Marriage à la Chicana

Marriage is the one thing Latinas look forward to with elation. This is understandable because of their conditioning. *"Cuando te cases . . ."* ["When you get married . . ."] is a daily sermon throughout their lives. Learn how to cook, iron, wash, sew, keep house and take care of children *para que estés lista cuando te cases* ["so when you get married you'll be prepared"]. Be thrifty, be an early riser, take care of your brothers and wait on and serve your papá *para que cuando te cases lo hagas bien* ["so when you get married you will do your chores well"]. Don't be lazy, don't complain, don't ask for anything *porque cuando te cases, tu marido se puede enojar* ["because if you do these things, your husband may get angry"]. *"Cuando te cases . . ."* love your husband as though he were a king and he'll be good to you. *"Cuando te cases . . ."* you'll live happily ever after. The *cuando te cases* sermons are endless.

On Track with Tradition

Weddings are a big thing for Latinas—the bigger the better. It's not unusual to see wedding entourages of eight couples or more. Once I attended a wedding with *twenty* couples as attendants. The bride's family, six sisters and three brothers, plus all her aunts and uncles were in it!

To this day, I remember the eighteen-year-old very naïve bride who remarked that she included everyone in her wedding so no one would feel left out. During the time she was planning her wedding, members of her immediate family were not getting along. She thought that if she invited everyone to be in the wedding, her family would be distracted from their problems and everything would be right again.

She confessed that she and her fiancé had wanted only a small quiet civil wedding, but when she mentioned these plans to her family, what she heard was, "You can't do that. You have to get married in church, wear a white dress, have a reception with lots of food and a big dance. You have to do it right, so that everyone will know about your wedding and will always remember it."

She explained to them that she and her fiancé had elected to forgo a big wedding—thinking it financially wasteful—and had decided to use their money for furniture instead. But pressure to get married in the traditional way came from *both* families and she and her fiancé were left without the strength or *courage* to fight back. The bride said, "I couldn't fight them all."

Bettina R. Flores

Will Latinas Ever Really Be Free?

Latinas get married at a very early age. The cultural attitude—the sooner the better—is based on the myth that real life starts and culminates with marriage. Worst of all, the Latina does not even imagine there is anything else *but* marriage. She goes directly from the domination of her father to the domination of her husband with almost no time in between for herself. She is denied the personal freedom to explore her own God-given potential.

Marrying young is common, acceptable, encouraged and historically based. Maria at fifteen unknowingly married a married man. That marriage was dissolved and she remarried at sixteen. Her story:

> I have nine aunts and uncles on my mother's side of the family and seven on my dad's. Among all my relatives, I never saw a married life that I admired. My grandmother married at eleven and immediately had two children. Her husband left her, so she remarried and had fifteen more.

The reward for postponing marriage is, basically, freedom. If a Latina graduated from high school at eighteen and didn't marry until twenty-four or later, she would have six years for self-analysis and self-development. During this "me" period she could learn about herself—what she liked and didn't like. She could sample college, adult education or correspondence courses. She could try a variety of jobs to earn and spend money for her whims. She could join clubs, attend lectures and travel. She could educate herself, study how-to books on her interests, subscribe to magazines and read several newspapers per day. She could become politically active, nurture friendships with Latinas and others, experience relationships with males, platonic or otherwise. She could do whatever she pleased! There is absolutely nothing wrong with spending some time on *me*. It is not selfish or self-centered; it is *self-caring*. It is vitally essential to "know thyself" and be in charge of your own self before you can be of any real value to others.

The *me* period is an interlude of personal growth. When the mind is open and receptive, the intake of fresh ideas is a miraculous thing. New information and new experiences stimulate new attitudes and beliefs. As a result, old thinking is easier to leave behind.

It is of paramount importance for Latinas to *do it*. Find your inner self—the person you really *want* to be, not the one you *ought* to be—and do it *before* you commit yourself to the encumbrance of matrimony. As any married woman can verify, once you're married your time is just not your own anymore. You may lose that inner self forever.

Marriage or Bust

There are reasons for getting married, but they should not include:

I want to get out of the house.

I'm pregnant.

I'm getting older.

Everyone else is.

I feel like it.

I'm in the mood for a wedding.

My mom wants me to settle down.

All my girlfriends are married.

He has a good job and can support me.

I won't be able to find anyone better.

He's nice enough.

I'm tired of being single.

I want a baby to take care of.

I want sex.

I want a man, period.

If you get married for any of the above reasons, you will probably soon regret it. Most likely, you will be unhappy and wish you could get out of the marriage.

If you're a Latina woman whose attitudes and beliefs reflect the traditional culture, you can't get out of the marriage for many reasons:

First, you might not recognize the problem, let alone admit it to yourself.

Second, you think that if you discuss the problem you'll be thought selfish and self-centered.

Third, you know that no one else, particularly your family, is concerned with your problem. It's not proper to air your dirty laundry to anyone.

Fourth, you saw your mother put up with much, much more, so you don't dare complain.

Fifth, you've been taught, "You made your bed, now lie in it." And silently, please.

Sixth, you have no money and no place to go.

Seventh, you have no job or job skills.

Eighth, you're afraid of your husband.

Ninth, you promised the church you'd be married forever.

Tenth, you think so little of yourself that your ultimate happiness is just not important enough for you to demand change.

You, the traditional Latina woman, have been conditioned, indoctrinated, manipulated and nailed to the cross like Christ himself, to suffer and to endure a life of sacrifice.

La Santita, aka the Invisible Woman

A married Latina who has aspired to the rank of Christ is called La Santita. We all know her, don't we? She's the Super-Latina whom everyone *pretends* to admire. She's the one who holds the family together, keeps order and peace, waits on her husband and family hand and foot twenty-four hours a day and always excuses her husband's behavior, even when he beats her or blows the family paycheck. And she never complains. Sound familiar?

La Santita makes sure that everyone else's needs are met while neglecting her own. On the surface she appears physically, psychologically and emotionally sound, but a close look at her eyes and the lines on her face reveal her tiredness, her secret burdens. La Santita appears happy. If one day she feels unhappy, she figures it is just her mood and doesn't mention it to anyone. She's a churchgoer who participates in church activities. From the minute she wakes up to her last tired breath at night she serves everyone. When she's depressed, no one knows, especially not herself. She accepts life as it is, believing that her condition and situation are normal. Her life is one of sacrifice and near slavery. She looks more like the maid than the woman of the house.

We all know many Santitas. They're very close to us. They're our mothers, sisters, aunts, cousins and friends who don't see that the La Santita role is a hurtful and self-destructive one. It is a martyrdom, stifling all opportunities for any self-development. In addition, it projects a negative stereotypical role model for children, both male and female.

Although I'm somewhat sympathetic toward Santitas, I am mostly disgusted and angry! When I see what's happening to them (especially the younger ones) I want to shake them and cry, "Look, can't you see what's happening to you here? You were not made to be a bondswoman! Do something! Change!"

But we know why she can't change. Her years of cultural conditioning keep her in her place. Well, if she won't change, others will.

A Latino friend of mine married an Anglo woman who later died in a car accident. Within a few years, he married another Anglo woman. I asked him why he married Anglos and he replied, "My mother was a Santita." He was afraid that if he married a Latina she would be just like his mother. He said he loved his mother but didn't respect her. When there was trouble in the house he recalled asking his mother, *"Mamá, ¿por qué dejas que papá te haga eso?"* ["Mother, why do you let father treat you so badly?"] And she replied, *"Pues, mi hijo, ¿qué puedo hacer?"* ["Well, son, what can I do?"] "I felt sorry for her," he told me. "She couldn't break out of her role because she was afraid to challenge her traditional position. I'm sure it was mostly out of fear and ignorance." He described his mother as the Virgin Mary type—pure, sweet, childlike. "But," he emphasized, "I didn't want to marry a traditional Latina, having her repeat my mother's role."

The Armor of Machismo and the Latina's Surrender

Machismo is rampant within Latino marriages. Machismo is that subtle but very strong force that keeps a Latina "in her place." Sometimes machismo is not so subtle. It can be a slap across the face, a punch in the jaw or a kick in the stomach. Machismo is the bastardly aura of the Latino husband who says, *"Aquí mando yo"* ["I'm the boss here and you will obey me"]. Machismo is an integral part of the Latino male. Because it is ingrained in him, he rarely operates without it. Macho men want to rule. They want all their needs—physical, emotional, psychological and spiritual—met at all times by "their woman." Being married to a macho is like being a slave to a king. Machismo attitudes extend from the kitchen to the bedroom and to the children; they persist unchanged generation after generation.

From the day a Latina starts her role as a wife, she is subjugated by machismo. She carries out her household chores without any assistance from her husband. She prepares his meals, does his laundry and manages his household. When her husband gets home from work, she's always there to greet him with dinner ready. If she's employed, she'll rush home to take care of him. She is desperate for his approval.

Machismo gives a man a privileged position. In the Latino culture, the traditional wife must always be home waiting for her husband to get home from work. If she isn't, he will demand to know why. He'll shout and rave at her as if she has committed a crime. Angrily, he'll remind her she is always to be there waiting for him.

He also tells her she's not to go anywhere during the day unless she gets his permission ahead of time. Meekly the Latina accepts her husband's authority, and the control/obedience cycle begins.

Macho husbands are mean, jealous and possessive. To cover up their insecurities and jealousies, they prey upon their wives by instilling fear in them. Linda, for example, lived it all:

> From the first day of our marriage my husband sat me down and told me what I could and could not do. I could not go anywhere or do anything without his permission.
>
> I didn't understand his attitude. I wanted to please him. I was young and deeply in love with him, so I did everything he said.
>
> But I couldn't even have coffee with my neighbors. Several times he called during the day and didn't find me home and boy did I catch hell! When friends or relatives came to visit me, I caught it again. He even posted a sign outside our front door saying NO VISITORS.
>
> I let him rule my life for twenty-seven years before I got the courage to divorce him.

We witness the armor of machismo and the Latina's surrender over and over. The classic everyday picture: Sara is making dinner, balancing and holding the baby with her left arm and stirring the pot of soup with her right. Mario is leaning against the kitchen sink telling Sara about his day. He walks to the kitchen table, sits down and says, *"Sara, tráeme un vaso de agua"* ["bring me a glass of water"]. Sara automatically puts down the spoon, rebalances the baby, goes to the cupboard for a glass, fills it with water and takes it to Mario.

Why didn't it occur to Mario that because Sara had her hands full, he should get his own water? Why didn't it occur to Sara to tell Mario to get it? Obviously, both are living their traditional roles. He commands; she obeys.

The Latina woman is trained to accept her husband's machismo program of *"dame ésto," "tráeme esto," "hazme ésto," "dame de comer," "vámonos"* ["get me this," "bring me that," "do this for me," "feed me," "let's go now"]. His commands plague her twenty-four hours a day, every day of her life! She is programmed to obey his orders.

When Latinas "play into machismo," they in turn teach their offspring that machismo is acceptable and right. I recall a visit with one of my friends about 5:30 P.M. one afternoon:

> We were playing pony rides with her two little girls when her husband arrived. My friend quickly bucked her daughter off her back, but the little girl, thinking we were still playing, scrambled back on.
>
> My friend shouted, "Get off, your father is home," but the little girl clung tightly to her neck. Angrily, my friend shouted louder, "I mean it, get off; I have to serve

your father," then yanked her daughter loose. Leaving her crying, my friend gave her husband a big kiss and said, "I have your dinner all ready for you."

Her husband hadn't had to say a word. His demeanor and body language said it all. All he had to do was walk in, wait (not very long) and he would have his wife where he wanted her, doting on him. How demeaning for my friend and her daughter to be sucked into his machismomania. How cowardly we are to fall prey to men like this.

What happens when a Latina gets sick? Does her husband put his machismo aside? Does he care for her? Is he sympathetic? Does he send or bring flowers? Call her from work?

Rarely.

A Latina doesn't dare take the time to be sick. She knows she must keep serving her husband and family without interruption because they expect it. In her mind, she's not important enough to be ill. Whether she is sick or healthy, her life is dictated by machismo. When she gives birth to a child and is still not feeling like her old self, she goes on as if the demanding care of the newborn did not add to her burden. Whether she's exhausted, emotionally drained or physically ill makes no difference. She accepts her misery as normal, refusing to complain or ask for help.

Personally, I've been such a heroine, of sorts. One week after the birth of my third child (I was thirty), I was out looking for a job. Ridiculous! I couldn't fit into any of my clothes, but I bought a dress two sizes bigger than normal, put on some new makeup and pretended I was ready for the working world.

I felt awful. My stitches from the episiotomy were painful. My full breasts felt like two-ton balloons and made me feel terribly self-conscious. Unable to handle the guilt of leaving my newborn with a baby-sitter I took him with me to job interviews. Mentally, I was frazzled.

My husband didn't notice any of this, of course, and I didn't mention it. Not once did he say, "Are you sure you're okay?" or "Are you feeling up to it so soon?" or "How are you going to manage?" My husband didn't tell me in so many words that I had to get back to work right away, but his worrying about our finances pressured me.

Looking back now, I wonder why I didn't admit to myself that I wasn't ready, physically or otherwise, to face the working world. Why didn't I have the *courage* to tell my husband, "I can't go back to work yet. We'll have to find other resources to tide us over until I can." Answer: I was culturally shackled and overanxious to please.

Even under normal circumstances, the childbearing years are hard on the Latina. She alone assumes her babies' twenty-four-hour care while her husband continues his machismo march for meals, laundry and personal attention.

Many poorer Latinas must obey their spouses regardless of circumstances. When I was a little girl picking grapes in the 100 + degree heat of California's San Joaquin Valley, I saw many Latinas picking on their knees, dragging their newborn infants along in small baskets.

One day I saw something much worse. I heard crying coming from a parked car so I went to investigate. It was a newborn infant, red as a beet, soaking in perspiration, chewing on its tiny-fisted hand and screaming its lungs out. No one was around. It had been left there, I presumed, while the mother worked. By the odor, it had been unattended for several hours. I changed it, gave it a dry sponge bath and looked futilely for a bottle. Unable to find one, I comforted the infant for a short while and then put it back down. It was the best a six-year-old could do. To this day I wonder if the baby survived the summer. I can't believe a mother would voluntarily take her newborn to the fields and leave it in the car in 100-degree weather. I've often wondered if she was ordered to.

The classic example of machismo occurs when the husband is absent from the home. The oldest son assumes his father's position almost instinctively. Whether he is fifteen or thirty-five years old is irrelevant. He plays the role with power. Because he is younger, stronger, more energetic and cockier, the son will often be worse than his father. He will rule over his mother and other family members unmercifully. Concha, an attractive divorced fifty-year-old, shares her home with her twenty-five-year-old son:

Angel runs my life, my business and my romantic relationships. He screens my mail, telephone calls and visitors. Without consulting me, he makes large withdrawals from the family business. If I confront him, he beats me.

Does Concha realize she has a macho son?

Oh yes. From the day my husband left, Angel took right over. I'm afraid of him just like I was of his father. Probably more because Angel is meaner. But I can't fight him any more than I could his father. I'm just waiting for him to get married and move out of the house. Then maybe I'll have peace.

Machismo also makes its debut socially. Have you ever conversed with Latino couples and noticed that when the wife starts talking, her husband interrupts? He corrects her and carries on the conversation for her. If and when she gets another chance to enter the conversation, she keeps her eyes on her husband as if to say, "Am I saying it right now, honey?" (She'd better; he's glaring at her anyway.)

At parties, macho husbands expect their wives to be conservative and demure. But they rarely fail to admire the other woman who is just the opposite. Anita, twenty-five, is a secretary. She relates:

> My husband says he married me because I was outgoing and bubbly. But at parties he scolds me for it. So I've toned myself down. But then he says, "Why don't you act more like So-and-so? She's so outgoing."

Patricia, twenty-nine, is a postal clerk. She admits:

> When I was married to Joe he always checked my clothes. I couldn't go anywhere if he didn't approve of what I had on. There were many times when he made me change, especially for dances and parties.

Gloria, barely twenty-one, says her plight is the worst:

> Going to parties with my husband is embarrassing and insulting. He gets so drunk, then starts telling everyone what a perfect and obedient wife I am. "See," he'll say,

"she'll sit there and wait for me while I dance with everyone else."

The most pathetic is the Latina who never talks, mingles or dances at social functions. She just sits, statuelike, by her partner. It makes one wonder why she bothered to step out at all. It makes one wonder what kind of hold her partner has on her.

Awaken! Know What Is Going on Around You!

Machismo, wherever and whenever, perpetuates the low self-esteem of Latinas. Machismo causes a male to:

order you about,

push you around,

make you feel stupid,

embarrass you,

chastise you,

abuse you

and

strip you of your right to personal dignity.

Accepting machismo from our fathers, husbands, sons, brothers, uncles and other men, because that's the way things are and have always been, is a Hispanic hang-up. As many herein have testified, it is *harmful*! When you allow yourself to be the victim of machismo attitudes and actions, you are encouraging your own self-degradation! Maybe, just maybe, one of the main reasons Latinas are not making it in the greater society is that after being dominated by their fathers, husbands, brothers and other males they have no self-esteem, no pride, no energy left to take on the demands of the outside world. When you have someone browbeating you at home—negating your skills, amputating your confidence, making you feel unworthy—there's no way you'll be able to function successfully in a competitive society. Your weakened personality, downgraded status and emotional strife carry over into whatever you attempt, whether it's a job, school or simple daily interactions.

Every Latina has the power to fight machismo by becoming *aware* of it and acquiring the *courage* to say "no more." It can be done in small steps or giant ones. Both work. By saying "no more" you'll preserve your self-esteem and dignity. Your feeling of self-worth will rise to new heights.

You-Know-What

Sex is still referred to by many Latinas as "you-know-what."
Latinas are naïve about sex. They see it as a duty and, therefore,
don't fake headaches too often. They view sex within marriage as
okay because the church says it's okay, but sex before marriage
makes them feel guilty.

The Hispanic Facts of Life

For Latinas, sexual activity is started and ended by the man. Lupe,
forty-one, married twenty years, puts it concisely:

> I didn't know anything about sex, so whatever he wanted
> to do, I let him. I didn't know any different, so whatever
> happened didn't matter. He was supposed to be satis-
> fied, not me.

Grace, twenty-seven, mother of three and pregnant again:

> I wish I knew how to turn Mike off without making him
> mad. Sometimes when I'm so tired I just want to get to
> sleep, he'll insist on "messing around." He'll persist and
> persist until, out of desperation for sleep, I'll give in, and
> pretend to enjoy it. I wish I knew how to handle him
> better.

One summer a friend of mine and her husband came for a weekend
visit. I had not seen her for a few years and was surprised to see
she had gained a great deal of weight and looked very matronly—at
thirty-six! After she hung up their clothes in my bedroom, she and
I sat on the bed and talked. When it grew late she said, "Well, I
better take my shower . . . just in case John wants to 'you-know-
what' tonight."

The words "in case John wants to" clanged in my ears! I was
shocked! My first thought, but what if you *don't* want to? My
second thought, she couldn't say the words "making love." I felt
sad for her.

What José Wants, José Gets

When I was in college and living in an apartment behind a gas
station, I'd occasionally go to the station to get a soda where Jesús,
fifty-ish, would strike up a conversation with me. His favorite topic
was sex. Invariably he'd end up telling me how wonderful his wife
was to him. One of his more memorable statements: "I have sex
with my wife every night. But," he tagged on, "I leave her alone

when she's on her period, so she can rest." I never knew if I should believe Jesús until the day I met his wife. Seeing how haggard and defeated she looked, I knew Jesús wasn't lying. She had had his thirteenth child and looked like only death could save her.

Sex is always presented to us only in relation to men's sexual needs. We're told that men have tremendous sex drives and insatiable sexual appetites. They forever need release and unless we satisfy their desires and needs, they will find satisfaction elsewhere. No one ever mentions our sex drive or that we matter at all. "Look pretty. Smell pretty. Always be ready. It's your duty. It might hurt a little at first but you'll get used to it. If you're good to your man, he'll take care of you." We were negotiable items before we got to the negotiating table! The Catholic Church, too, teaches us that woman was made for man and that "obedient sex" is God's will—for procreation, of course.

The Hidden Meanings of Sex

Sex, sex, sex. Love, love, love. All of us get megadoses of these overrated fantasies every day of our lives! Movies, television, books, magazines, billboards and especially love songs constantly indoctrinate us with strong love emotions until we're supersaturated. Women often go around like lovesick puppies, wearing their hearts on their sleeves, thinking only with their revved-up emotions, living and breathing only for *him*. Careful, ladies. Too much of this hot stuff can prevent you from operating sensibly.

Don't be a romantic all the time (not even most of the time) because this attitude can dominate your thinking and override your ability to make decisions. Keep in mind that for men, the passion and excitement of sex is more physical than emotional. The male sex drive is not romantic in nature but for women it is "love, love, love." This is where we get into trouble. A good way to stay out of this kind of trouble is to see and understand romance, love and sex separately.

Gushing romance and true love are two different things. Romance is unrelated to reality. It means dates, gifts, long drives, love songs, butterfly feelings and sexual anxiety. Romance is walking on air, being on cloud nine and being swept off your feet. It's fun, wonderful and exciting. Even lovers' quarrels heighten the passion of romance. All of this is, of course, temporary. Eventually even the best bubble bursts. So what happens when it's all over? What happens when the flattery and courting end and the "hots" get "cold"? Ask yourself then, what's left? Sometimes nothing. Sometimes romance matures into love.

Love doesn't require the constant hullabaloo of romance. Love is founded on reality. It's having both feet firmly on the ground, being able to see your partner, yourself and the relationship clearly. You have your individual life to live; your partner has his. The love you share should support, not dominate, your lives.

Since sex plays a big a part in romance *and* love, you might be interested in some basic facts.

First, firmly believe that sex is okay. Second, know that sex should not be a one-way affair. You should be a voluntary participant, getting your share of the pleasure when and how you want it. Third, no one, absolutely no one but you (not even the church) knows how much or how little sex you need. Fourth, you don't have to commit yourself to a lifetime of sex if it doesn't suit you. You have the right to say no. Fifth and most important, not all sex is related to love.

There are many reasons for sex.

Our first sexual experience results from a variety of motives like curiosity, duty, fear, pleasure and cooperation. Like anything attempted for the first time, however, sex can also be a failure, a frustrating experience, even a complete let-down. We expect to see brilliant stars and to be taken to heights of ecstasy. We expect tenderness, adoration, tingly feelings and approval. These expectations are not unrealistic, but unless your partner has the same feelings, your expectations may not be met. The issue, however, is that as you become more experienced with sex, you need to see and understand the reasons for it. If you don't, your emotional well-being will always be at risk!

Sex as Duty   The least valid reason for having sex is to do it *only* for someone else's pleasure. Allowing this to happen is allowing yourself to be coerced and prostituted. You are left powerless. This kind of sex is accompanied by vicious contempt and is a loud message saying, "I have power over you. You are my property." Men who demand this kind of sex don't care about women. They perceive them as chattel and feel that they own them, body and soul. When a man dominates a woman in bed, you can be sure he has the power to make the rest of her life a living hell! To submit yourself to such "duty" is to subordinate your self-esteem. All other areas of your life are negatively affected.

Sex as Possession   Many women feel they can hang on to men through sex. Women who believe this think very little of themselves. They feel they have nothing else to offer. Obviously feeling insecure, they use sex to control their relationships.

Sex for Love   Sex for love sounds romantic as well as old-fashioned. For example, men have always known that women nearly always fall for the "Yes, I love you, now let's go to bed" line. Because many women believe they have to be "in love," they perceive love and sex as the same thing. Naturally, men take advantage of this. Women think sex will bring them love; consequently they strive to give their partners sexual satisfaction. Sex as love can be an illusion. How much a man truly loves you should not be measured in bed, because in bed is the one place he'll always say, "Yes, of course, I love you." Sex itself rarely brings love, although it has been responsible for some lovely dinners.

Sex for Intimacy   Some people think sex automatically brings people closer together emotionally. But physical intimacy does not mean emotional intimacy. Real intimacy involves two people really getting to know each other and this takes a lot of time and talking.

Sex for Reassurance   People whose primary purpose in sex is to make as many conquests as possible without emotionally involving themselves in a relationship, usually are the Don Juans and the Doña Juanitas acting to overcome feelings of inferiority to feel more attractive and desirable and to prove their sexual adequacy.

Sex for Self-esteem   Since sex is so important in our society, being good at it is obviously important too. Some people see sex as a skill to be perfected, like a good game of golf.

Sex as Hostility   A sexually hostile person becomes angry and ridicules you if you refuse to have sex. Men are accused of being impotent or gay, women of being frigid. These are angry people although their anger has nothing to do with you.

Sex as a Weapon   Sexually attractive people can use sex as a tool for manipulation to acquire power, status, money and more. The sexual harassment of women is a good example. Some women use their sexuality to manipulate men.

Getting Your Share Your Way

All this makes a lot of sense to me. Because I am an individual with my own attitudes, beliefs and experiences, I've found my own niche in regard to sex. I think sex is neither a "must have" (no one ever died from not having it) or a "no-no" (he won't respect me in the morning). To me, it falls somewhere in between, among my other priorities. Like many other things, sex is what you make it. I am a very sexual person. My sexual activities are governed by my personal needs, as well as my consent, in cooperation with my husband. For me, sexual fulfillment comes in diverse forms. Sometimes it's strictly biological, sometimes emotional with a need to be caressed, soothed and comforted, sometimes a desire to give pleasure and sometimes total intimacy—a strong and sincere connection with him on all levels. Above all, I value my body as sacred. It is dainty and fragile and it always deserves to be handled with care. So I make sure he is aware of this all the time. Under no circumstances would I ever allow myself to be sexually mistreated.

What can you do? Get in touch with your own sexual attitudes that stem from your cultural and religious conditioning. Examine them. Do they fit in with how you really feel? Think. Within your lifestyle, does sex enhance or diminish your zest for living? Is the sex you're having now what you dreamed it would be? What changes in your thinking or behavior would make sex more enjoyable for you? When you put sex into perspective, you'll have a better chance of putting the other parts of your life in order as well. Why? Because sex, so often confused with love, entangles the emotions to the point that it affects everything you do. If you feel you need some formal sex education, be brave and get it! If you are sexually experienced and mature but afraid to challenge your traditional role, a scoop of *courage* may be all you need.

La Familia:
Just the Ten of Us

*T*he pill has been out since the sixties, but according to statistics Latinas are having 2.9 children, which is significantly higher than the average 1.8 for other women in the general population.

Consequently, Latinos are the fastest-growing group in the United States and destined to be the largest by the turn of the century. Many people say this is terrific because it gives us great political power. These people, however, just happen to be men, and I disagree with them. First, political power is not going to be handed to us just because we're large in numbers. (It could be, however, if we would get to the polls and vote.) Second, political power is based on economics and Latinos have yet to build a strong economic base. And as much as it hurts me to say this, overall things are pretty unsatisfactory for us. In a 1993 United Nations survey that measured life educational levels and basic purchasing power, Latinos in the United States were ranked in thirty-fifth place, about the same level as Latvians. Third, because most Latinos are economically deprived, their priority is keeping food in their mouths and roofs over their heads—not politics. Obviously, since men don't get pregnant, don't have babies and don't have to care for children, they can afford to endorse the concept of large Latino populations. The question is, are *Latinas* going to continue producing large families just to support the political hopes of men?

Until we wise up, the question is a moot one because no matter who says what, we are religiously, culturally and traditionally conditioned to having many children. I probably knew when I was four years old that I was going to have a big family. It was unavoidable. I was the youngest of seven children. Besides my sisters and brothers, I was always surrounded by my aunts', uncles' and cousins' children. Babies, children and mothers everywhere, all the time! So, for me, it was only natural that I would also have many children.

More important, there was *never* anything said to the contrary. It was always, "You'll have lots of children when you get married." Not ever one word of, "Take care that you don't have too many children." Small families are not common in the Latino culture, and couples without children are rare.

My husband and I could never have said to each other, "Let's not have any children." Our belief system said, "Get married and have a big family. God will bless you and you'll be happy."

Marriage and children are practically a must within the Latino culture. Because indoctrination starts early, Latinas marry young, have many children and get stuck early. Altering the way we've learned to live is not easy. I know. I tried.

How Cultural and Religious Conditioning
Keeps Us Pregnant Again and Again

I was on and off the pill often, but my belief in birth control was not as strong as my large-family conditioning. I even tried another route. Immediately after the birth of my second child (I was twenty-six), I bravely and cheerfully agreed to have a tubal ligation. The feeling was exhilarating and many ideas ran through my mind. With fewer children to support and care for, I would have fewer responsibilities and more opportunities for a career outside the home, more money in my pocket for pleasures like a new car and nice clothes, sexual freedom, and abundant physical and mental energy for personal interests. Then, too, I'd stay youthful instead of being worn out by the exhausting demands of motherhood.

Alas, it was only a dream.

As I was waiting to go into surgery, something made me change my mind. I told the doctor, "I can't do this." I wanted to, but couldn't. I retreated to my room crying and pulled the warm covers over my head. I'm sure this was symbolic of a desire to be safely back in the familiar cocoon.

Changing my mind kept me in line with everything I had learned and accepted. The "something" stopping me was a combination of many influences: my cultural large-family conditioning, my inability to accept permanent birth control as an advantage of life, my need to have acceptance within my group, my instincts for survival and my fear of burning in hell, as I'd been taught by the Catholic Church.

Regardless, the practice of having more children than we want, or can manage or afford, strongly diminishes the Latina's opportunity for anything more than a life of motherhood. If motherhood is her choice, fine, but often motherhood is synonymous with martyrdom, because most Latino fathers do not actively participate in parenting. The Latina does it all. Whoever said "Parenting is a mother's life sentence with no parole" hit the nail on the head.

When will we cease having large families? That's a tough question to answer. The pill and other contraceptives have been out for decades. How much longer can Latinas, myself included, go on saying, "It was unavoidable. Birth control was not a part of my upbringing." Will planned parenthood continue to escape us in generations to come?

Looking back, I consider myself lucky, as opposed to smart, for having had only four children; three of my sisters' and both of my brothers' families mushroomed into fives and sixes. A fourth sister, a devout Catholic, had eight children and actually yearned for twelve.

Latinas assume that being pregnant is one of the greatest things that can happen to them and, therefore, they should be thankful. Because of our cultural conditioning, we find ourselves rationalizing: "It's okay to get pregnant without thinking or planning, because that's what I'm supposed to be doing. It is expected and acceptable. I'll be praised for it."

Laura, a thirty-two-year-old housewife, says every time she got pregnant she became a queen. Her conversations with relatives went like this:

¿Estás embarazada?   Are you pregnant?

Sí.   Yes.

71

Ay, ¡qué mujer tan linda!	Oh, you're lovely.
Me encanta ver a mujeres embarazadas.	I love to see women pregnant.
Dios debe de quererte mucho.	God must truly love you.
Ay, ¡qué bueno!	This is good.
Felicidades.	Congratulations.
Tú eres una reina.	You are a queen.

From then on Laura was someone special. She was a queen. If someone else in the family became pregnant, she also became a queen. But by her fourth pregnancy Laura felt different:

> I didn't feel like a queen at all. Another baby meant a lot more work, much tighter purse strings and getting fat all over again!

Baby Bliss or Baby Blues?

Sure, babies are cute, and compared with grown children, easy to care for. But when a new baby comes along every year, year after year, the pitter-patter of tiny feet may result in more than you can handle. If you're organized, patient and a *Chata* ["happy home-maker"] type who loves caring for children and doesn't have to work outside the home, you'll keep yourself and your large family going merrily along. If you're not, however, you're likely to be in the coma of depression common to many Latinas. Sheila, only thirty-five, takes two tranquilizers during the day and a sleeping pill at night for her nerves. She's married but feels she's raising her eight children—3, 5, 6, 7, 8, 9, 11, 14—alone:

> Just getting them off to school every day wears me out. And when I have to listen to their lists of needs and wants, I run for a tranquilizer. My husband doesn't make much money, so when he comes home he gets his beer and sits. Asking him to help me makes things worse. I'm young, but I feel old and trapped.

Delia, thirty, had five children in a row and her husband, Ray, always pitched in. But things changed. She says:

> When we first started having our babies we were so happy. Now the kids are bigger and suddenly they're my kids only. Ray says he loves them but doesn't want to put up with them. The kids make me so nervous I cry a lot. Now I don't know why I had so many kids in the first place.

Clara, thirty-nine, has nine kids and a husband who's been unemployed most of their married life. She complains:

> I live in a stupor. I feel sick most of the time and when I go to the doctor he says, "Nothing is wrong with you—you're depressed." He tells me to go home and take care of my problems. But I don't know how or where to start. When I go see Father John he says, "Have faith. God will provide."

Laura, only twenty, already has three children but doesn't want to care for them anymore. She says:

> I'm too young to be stuck mothering. I want to be out with my friends, having a good time. When we divorced, I gave Jess the kids. I'll probably remarry and have more cute babies anyway.

As the family and its demands grow, the initial dream of a large, close family having fun slowly disappears. The children become work and more work and more work. You can stop to wonder what happened, but it's too late. You can't send the children back, can you? When you realize you are practically rearing them by yourself, you grow weary. Hubby may be around, but he leaves all the family matters to you. When the children start growing up, start talking back, wandering in the streets and being exposed to alcohol, drugs, crime and violence, the pressure and stress zap *you*. The first adolescent verbal attack like "Fuck you, Mom!" devastates you. You can't believe that these are your sweet babies of yesteryear.

What happens when you find yourself overwhelmed by the responsibilities of parenting? Your ability to function in a normal, healthy manner is at real risk. Stress sets in. You start to feel blue, trapped and unable to cope.

The more children you have, the heavier the load of responsibility you must bear, the more expensive life will be and the more sacrifices you will be forced to make.

Letting Maternal Instincts Devour Us

There is in all of us mujeres a maternal instinct ordering us to take care of others before we take care of ourselves. Proof? How many times do we go out and buy what the children want but absolutely nothing for ourselves? Are you wearing the latest fashion—be it a sweat shirt or a piece of new fad jewelry? I'll bet your children are. How many pair of panties do you own? How many does your daughter have? The ratio is probably one to four. Here's my truth: I buy my underwear at Thrifty's; my daughter gets hers at Macy's. Why is money available for their activities but not for ours? How is it hubby gets a regular beer budget, but we don't get our hair or nails done regularly? When hubby goes out with the boys, do we think about going to the movies or shopping with the girls? No. We stay home with the kids.

Our maternal instinct tells us that they need more than we do. We are the nurturers. We nurture everyone but ourselves. This happens because we don't see ourselves as important or deserving enough to give ourselves the same privileges. Our maternal instincts govern us. The fight to conquer this dominating "I love them more than me" instinct is an ongoing one. The more children you have, the harder it is to control.

Sacrificing your needs and desires for your children is not healthy. As the children grow bigger and more expensive, there will be *years* and *years* of self-sacrifice taking you further down in status and self-esteem. You're bound to get depressed and maybe physically ill.

Depression is a very real illness. It appears in many forms: oversleeping or sleeplessness, hopelessness, moodiness, anxiety attacks, listlessness, overeating or inability to eat, loss of energy and undue fatigue. Depression is like having the lights in your head turned off. You can't see your way clearly through anything. You can't handle anything. When it continues over a long period of time, depression can weaken and even destroy a healthy body and mind.

The more depression sets in, the less energy you'll have and the deeper you'll fall into the "I'm not worth it" syndrome. You'll stop combing your hair. You'll stop wearing makeup. You'll become a bathrobeaholic. This in turn will create new stress and will probably make you gain weight. Now because you feel fat, ugly and broke, you'll drop out, stay home, do nothing and slumber into an early old age. Of course, while all this is happening, your children are watching and learning how to live just like you.

All these things can and do happen because we close our eyes to the real issue: We do not see motherhood as work. Very few of us want to admit it and fewer of us dare mention it. Why? Such an admission would be complaining, and to complain would mean that we are not good, capable mothers. Let's face it, no one says "I'm going to have a baby and I'm going to have a lot of work to do." Instead we hear, "I'm going to have a baby. I'm so happy." *¡Por Dios!* What is wrong with our thinking? Raising children is one of the hardest jobs in the world and it's time to admit it. When we face this fact, perhaps we will learn to have fewer children.

The practice of having too many children totally hinders the Latina. Burned out by her maternal burdens, she can't see the horizon of hope in the outside world because she is too busy looking at the ground to see if her children are still at her feet!

El último consejo ["the last word"]: Years ago an eighty-year-old *abuelita* ["grandmother"] gave me the ultimate warning that made the hair on my neck stand up. At a family picnic, she asked to hold my newborn daughter. Cradling her warmly in her frail arms, she said, *"Que peligroso. Nunca se quitan las ganas."* ["This is dangerous. You keep wanting to have them."]

Careful, careful . . .

Getting Smart with Planned Parenthood

It's time for the Latina to ask herself some questions.

> Do I really want to have a child?
>
> Am I physically, mentally and financially ready for such responsibility?
>
> Can I afford a child?
>
> How will this child fit in with the other things I want to do with my life?
>
> My husband says he'll help, but can I really count on him?
>
> Will this child be a burden or a blessing?

Ignoring birth control results in pregnancy. Pregnancies (whether one or twenty) are very serious. Once a woman becomes pregnant, she is forever changed. Too often we see Latinas in poor health and totally depressed during their pregnancies. Too often we see a very young Latina with several children skipping in front of her, another toddling alongside and yet another in her arms. Look closely in any Latino neighborhood, in barrio shopping districts or in any county medical facility where poor women have to go for services and I doubt you'll see any Latinas who look like queens!

77

I'm not saying we should stop having babies or that we shouldn't be joyous about it. I am saying exactly what I said about sex. We need to put childbearing in perspective, use a degree of control and see how children fit in with the other parts of our lives and our future.

Although I love all four of my children dearly, my fourth pregnancy (unplanned) was extremely upsetting. My husband was an unemployed student and my salary was all we had. We were struggling with life in a new city and the pregnancy made things much harder. After the birth, I knew if we didn't start using a reliable and permanent birth control method, I would get pregnant *again* and *again*. I feared it so much that I refused to have sex. This, of course, caused a great deal of friction, but it started us thinking about not having any more children . . . and about a vasectomy.

I had already tried to get my tubes tied and couldn't go through with it. There's a big difference, however, between a tubal ligation and a vasectomy. A tubal ligation requires general anesthetic (being put to sleep), hospitalization and has a longer healing time. It is also permanent. A vasectomy is an outpatient procedure and can be done in the doctor's office with a local anesthetic. It is faster, safer and the healing time is shorter. The risk is so minimal the procedure is often compared to a trip to the dentist. A vasectomy has the possibility, although not the certainty, of being reversed.

When I suggested to my husband that he have a vasectomy, he refused. He gave me (but mostly himself) every reason he couldn't go through with it:

I'm too young.

What if I lose the kids or you?

What if we want more kids later on?

We can use other birth control methods.

Why don't you get your tubes tied?

What if I lose my virility?

You won't see me as a whole man.

God might punish me.

His rationalizations went on and on. Underneath it all, what was really bothering him was the thought that he would lose his manliness. His machismo was at risk!

A year later and through the help of some counseling he decided to have the vasectomy. Once it was done, we enjoyed a tremendous amount of sexual freedom. We felt relief that our family was finally complete and optimism that our future would be brighter. A great burden had been lifted from us.

It's a form of *courage* to be able to admit that your feelings don't always match the circumstances of your life. If you are pregnant and unhappy about the pregnancy, admit it to yourself and learn from it. This is much healthier than being unhappy about it and pretending to be full of joy. Lying to yourself is the worst type of oppression. Your attitude toward pregnancy is just as much a birth control device as the pill or any other contraceptive method is. Think about this.

Pressing my husband to have a vasectomy was more than an act of *courage.* It was an act of survival for my body, my spirit and my future. When I became aware and truly believed that I could not be a good mother to any more children, I found the *courage* to do something about it.

Religion:
Reality or Repression?

*T*raditionally, most Latinas are loyal, practicing Catholics. Growing up Catholic is as much a part of us as growing up Latina. Because of this, we accept the church and its teachings the same way we accept our traditional and cultural practices—wholeheartedly. Our church and our culture have this in common: They both require *obedience.*

As a result of this total and oppressive demand for obedience, there is a suffocating burden of church-induced guilt among Catholic Latinas. By the church's own definition, a good Roman Catholic is one who is obedient and subservient.

Let's see. The Latina *obeys* her father,

obeys her mother,

obeys her brothers,

obeys her relatives,

and on top of it all,

obeys her church!

No wonder the Latina can't make it in the competitive outside world. She is conditioned to follow orders. Somewhere, somehow, sometime, the Latina must become aware of all the forces paralyzing her mind.

Religion or Repression?

The Catholic Church teaches that God is the center of the universe and our true fulfillment is to gain a place in heaven next to Him.

QUESTION:	*Who made you?*
ANSWER:	*God made me.*
QUESTION:	*Why did God make you?*
ANSWER:	*To go to heaven.*

Within Catholic Church doctrines, getting to heaven is heavily emphasized. As a result, many Latinas are convinced that while you are on Earth you are not worth much because you are just earning the greater glory of heaven. These teachings give *you* a negative self-image but give the church a hold on your thinking, your behavior and your happiness. Lucy, twenty-five, a fragile and gentle mother of three, remembers this from her Catholic upbringing:

> Live your life as good as you can so you will go to heaven. Participate in confession, attend mass on Sunday, receive

communion and the sacraments, say your rosary often and pray for God's love and you *might* go to heaven were my constant messages. And if I didn't do all these things faithfully I would feel so *guilty* I was sure something bad was going to happen to me.

Ramona, twenty-one, a hearty factory worker recalls:

Striving to reach heaven always seemed like an uphill battle for me. No matter *how* good I was, I was always in doubt that I would reach heaven. Compared to the nuns, I felt so imperfect and I swear, they'd rub it in.

Kathy, eighteen and barely out of high school, still remembers the nuns' voices:

If you don't do "this and that" you won't go to heaven. The problem was that "this and that" was a mile long. The funny thing is, the nuns rarely inspired us to *want* to go to heaven. They just threatened. If we didn't do things their way, we would be sure not to get there.

At thirty-four, Joyce started to question her religious upbringing:

I began to wonder why so much importance was placed on the afterlife. I often wondered why we had to suffer on Earth in order to reach heaven. I was so brainwashed I couldn't even conceive that there could be a heaven on

Earth; that is, being happy without suffering. I think a lot
of us suffer because the church says we must.

And how do you get to heaven? According to the Catholic Church,
you can only get to heaven by being good; that is, by not sinning.
The problem is that to the Catholic Church almost *everything* is a
sin. Even newborn infants are born with original sin and have to
be saved through baptism. And who saves them? Why, the Catholic Church, of course. For many people, accusing newborn infants
of carrying the sin of Adam and Eve is beyond all sensible reasoning
and an example of a negative type of religion. Starting life on the
wrong side of the tracks, being taught to believe that you're unworthy, then being led to suffer the guilt of a sinner would demoral-
ize the best of us. To teach that almost everything in life is sinful
is to fill people with dread. The Catholic Church bombards its
members with threats of eternal damnation.

"Forgive me, Father, for I have sinned . . ." "Through my
fault, through my most grievous fault . . ." "O my God, I am
heartily sorry . . ." "Pray for us sinners, now and . . ." "I detest
all my sins because . . ." "O Lord, I am not worthy . . ." These are
some of the common Catholic prayers that reinforce our conviction
that we are indeed sinners. Most of us have sinned throughout our
lives:

IN CHILDHOOD

"I told my sister to shut up."

"I stuck my tongue out at my mother when her back was
turned."

"I found a nickel and didn't turn it in."

IN ADOLESCENCE

"A friend had a dirty picture and I looked at it for ten seconds."

"I missed mass because I couldn't find my shoe."

"I wore a tight sweater to the dance and the boys stared at me."

IN ADULTHOOD

"I disobeyed my husband."

"I spent household money on a new dress."

"I spoke badly about my husband's drinking buddies."

"I use a birth control device."

The Catholic Church warns you: If you commit any of the above sins and die without confession, you will probably spend years in purgatory or maybe even hell. Life on Earth is equally threatening. If you were raised Catholic you are probably *preoccupied with sin,* because the Catholic Church teaches you to *worry* about every little thing you do. You live thinking, "Now, was that a venial or a mortal sin? I wonder if I should confess that." Then you worry about how severe your penance will be. You even worry whether you'll remember to confess *all* your sins. Maybe you should make a list, because if you forget some and take communion it's another sin. Guilt, guilt and more guilt.

In the Catholic Church, you don't have to actually commit the sin; you just have to think about it and you're guilty. Per its teachings, "The *near* occasion of sin is always tempting you—the sinner." The other dimension of sinning that really brings on a heavy guilt trip, as if hell weren't enough, is that when you sin, you increase Christ's suffering. You are taught that you not only hurt yourself, but also injure another. How mean, insensitive and uncaring you are. The sisters were right after all. We really are bad.

When you grow up Catholic, you have very few *free-thinking* moments. With your programmed vulnerability to the hazards of sinning, energy for positive thinking stays on the back burner. Even when you find conflicting ideas in the church's teachings, you feel helpless to do anything about it. If you question anything, you get answers like "Those are the mysteries of the faith." If you're the nervy type you might ask, "Why is sex a mystery, Sister?" And, *wham,* the old ruler almost breaks your knuckles.

Birth Control Is Whose Right?

What about sex and Catholicism? When you ask Latinas what the Catholic Church taught them about sex, their answers are:

> The Catholic Church taught me zero. But in Sunday sermons Father would sometimes refer to the "wife's duty," implying that a wife should treat her husband right.

> In my day as a teenager, necking and kissing were considered serious sexual play and whenever I did it, I remember praying to my guardian angel to save me.

We were taught that our bodies were temples of the Holy Ghost.

They told me to stay pure like the Virgin Mary.

If I didn't stay a virgin, I couldn't get married in white.

This kind of teaching explains why, after she marries and begins her role as a "dutiful" wife, the Catholic Latina makes frequent trips "to go see Father." She may ask him openly or she may use the confessional to ask the priest what exactly are the church-approved parameters of her sexual responsibility. Although she may find pleasure in being dutiful, she also suffers from guilt. If she feels sexually inadequate, she'll feel even more guilty. Latinas habitually run to go see Father to unburden their problems but rarely have them solved. For the most part, Father offers one perfect solution: Obey, be a dutiful wife and carry out God's will.

The one thing the Catholic Church has vigorously taught is there shall be no birth control. Judging by the number of children Latinas have, this church law works quite well. But think about this, mujeres, *when the Catholic Church tells you what you can and cannot do with your body, it is saying your body is not your own!* To date, the church still sanctions only the rhythm method of birth control. In fact, all "the pelvic issues" (as they are referred to by the Vatican)—birth control, abortion, sterilization, premarital sex and what to do about Catholic gays—remains in tortuous debate. The celibacy policy for priests is another unresolved issue. In the past twenty years more than ten thousand priests have left the church to marry! The Vatican maintains its seemingly illogical stance despite this fact and the fact that eleven of the twelve apostles were married.

Sexism—Where Are All the Altar Girls?

A part of the church that has not been heard from during its two-thousand-year history: women! Today there are deeply devout religious women who want to be more than nuns, who want to be priests. Many of them are fighting strongly *for* equality. And if the Catholic Church isn't listening, Protestant churches are. Of some sixty thousand Catholic nuns, one third have left the convent. One half of those remaining are over sixty years of age. Does the church care? Not according to Auxiliary Bishop of New York Austin B. Vaughn, who says, "If the world lasts until the year two thousand, twenty thousand or two million, there will be a Catholic Church and it will still have an all-male clergy. A woman priest is as impossible as it is for me to have a baby." Just as sexism stalks our culture, sexism also stalks the Catholic Church. Ever wonder why there are no altar girls?

Time for a New Religion!

As the struggle for change is occurring within the church, the time has come for Latinas to face the mental abuse of Catholicism and to consider change. It may well be time for a new religion. More important, Latinas must face the fact that religion is man-made. The rules and regulations, the practices thrown upon you and the burdensome threats all have a single purpose—to control your body, mind and soul. Religion is control, period.

It is possible to have faith without the concept of sin. You can still love and believe in God and be a true Christian without subjecting yourself to an institution's psychological coercion. Many people don't have a church yet still keep their spirituality, their love of God, their guiding consciences and their moral standards. They are able to do so because they use their God-given minds to function self-reliantly without fear of retribution. Keep in mind that to rely solely on God is to transfer the responsibility for yourself to Him. Christ Himself was self-reliant and urged His followers to be. He did not intend for His teachings to be misused for power, authoritarianism, dominance and manipulation. Any Latina who suffers from religious persecution must wake up, take notice and revamp her thinking with calm and deliberate *courage*!

There's a visible, obvious correlation between being Catholic, being Latina and being poor. Why this is so should be examined and questioned by every impoverished Latina. Lack of education and lack of job skills are some of the causes of poverty, but religious beliefs can be even more damaging. Psychological attitudes can make the primary difference in winning the war against poverty, especially cyclical poverty.

What you believe determines how you act and carry out your life. Examine these religious beliefs:

Poverty is a virtue.

To suffer like Christ is to be Christ-like.

Blessed are the poor.

The poor are favored by God.

In God's eyes, I must be undeserving—a sinner—otherwise He would be more generous with me.

It's okay to be poor and without food, housing, health care or other vital resources because God will provide for me in heaven.

To complain of one's status is to argue with God (a sin) that you are dissatisfied with what He has given you (another sin).

Si Dios quiere ["If God wills it"].

When you believe these doctrines, you program yourself to accept them as reality. The more repetitious the messages, the more effectively the mind absorbs and obeys them. Those thirty- or sixty-second commercials on television come on repeatedly so that their messages will be fixed in your mind. They are so effective that advertisers think nothing of spending billions of dollars to program your buying.

The same principle applies to your religious conditioning. You receive and learn poverty messages from childhood. Your environment reinforces them. Unless you get some inkling that your life doesn't have to be one of deprivation, you believe, accept and are stuck in poverty!

Gloom and Doom in Patron Saints

Another religious practice that reinforces the acceptance of continual suffering and poverty is the use of the home altar. The statues of Christ on the crucifix, the Sacred Heart of Jesus or the Virgin of Guadalupe are popular symbols of Catholicism. They are also reminders of humility, sacrifice and suffering. They serve to remind you: "See, Christ suffered for you; now you should suffer for Him." It's a catch-22. You suffer from poverty yet the statues represent worse suffering, making yours seem insignificant by comparison. Hence you reason, "Why should I complain about my poverty when Christ suffered so much for me? I shouldn't ask for more." You accept poverty and suffering as your cross to bear.

Throughout their lives, Latinas (poorest of Americans) absorb repeated messages from these altars. A lifetime of negative inspiration can only produce negative results. It takes a lot of positive mental energy and motivation to beat poverty. The statues of the home altar, unfortunately, do not spark either one.

What would?

By comparison, successful wealthy people almost always have symbols of prosperity and accomplishment in their environment. They have busts, paintings, plaques, trophies, awards, books, videos, cassettes, posters and other motivational things to remind themselves of their success goals. They use their symbols to fix in their minds that they are entitled to achieve success. Contrary to what the Catholic Church has taught us, there is nothing spiritual or Christ-like about poverty. Christ himself was not poor. He was the son of a carpenter in times when a carpenter held a position of status. Christ's robe was made from the finest cloth. Jesus preached prosperity, not poverty. Remember that!

The Rise and Fall of Latino Catholicism

Are you thinking it is heretical, disrespectful, even sinful for me to write this way? Well, I departed from the guilt of Catholicism a long time ago. There comes a time in everyone's life when she must open her eyes, really open them, to see. Then, of course, you have to gather some *courage* to change what isn't right for you anymore. This happened to me when I was fourteen.

I was poor as a child. I suffered. I saw my mother, a widow with seven kids and a meager welfare check, suffer. I saw everyone around me suffer, not really certain where their next meal would come from. Still the smothering Catholic Church came after us when we failed to attend catechism and mass and vigorously insisted that our poverty was the will of God. We reacted to this by trying even harder, getting to mass more often, observing the Holy Days of Obligation and participating in more church activities. It didn't help much. Things remained the same.

During my freshman year in high school one incident changed my way of thinking. Since my mother was unable to pay for my Catholic school education, I worked at the convent for my tuition. One Saturday I was told to shell walnuts. For six boring, miserable hours I sat on the floor and shelled bushels of walnuts. The more tedious the job became, the angrier I got. Having come from the eighth grade with an almost A average and doing the same level of work in my freshman year, I thought that I should not be doing such work. I should have an office job after school, like the rest of the girls in my class. After thinking it through, I got the *courage* to ask Sister about it. She said no.

In homeroom the following Monday, Sister Agnes gave a lecture on being humble and practicing humility, all the time staring me down with her accusing eyes. "Jesus," she said, "was humble. What little we're asked to do we should do lovingly." She then added, "Humility is a Christ-like virtue." (Guilt and more guilt.)

Confused, I decided to look up the words "humility" and "humble." I wanted to be sure I knew what Sister meant.

humble: having or showing a consciousness of one's defects or shortcomings, not proud, not self-assertive; low in condition, rank or position; lowly, unpretentious.

humility: the state or quality of being humble; absence of pride or self-assertion.

Whoa! Sister *wanted* me to be humble? The wheels in my head started spinning. I could hardly believe Sister saw this quality as something good, especially for me! After all, wasn't I going to a "good" school and getting "good" grades so I could have "pride" in myself, so I could better myself and have status as an adult? I was born with "defects or shortcomings" but I was trying to overcome them through education and God's guidance. Without pride I couldn't make it in their racist, rich, holier-than-thou school. Just to compete with the lily-white blond-haired blue-eyed rich girls took extraordinary amounts of energy, every single day.

Sister, by lecturing me to practice humility, was in essence telling me to stay in my lowly position. Subtly and under the auspices of Jesus Christ, she was informing me that I must accept her vision of my destiny.

That did it! I suddenly recognized the condescending dogma of the Catholic Church for what it was: a means of controlling us. By teaching obedience and inducing guilt, the nuns and priests kept us in our places. My era of subservience to the Catholic Church ended!

I spent the remainder of the school year boldly agitating God's humble servant, Sister Agnes. She apparently forgave me for my sins, for at the end of the year she wrote in my yearbook, "God love you, Firecracker Bettina." (Guilt and more guilt.)

Dominus vobiscum. Et cum spiritu tuo. Granted, the church has changed considerably since my freshman days. The format and language of the mass have changed, the priests say mass facing the congregation, nuns wear modern dress, women aren't required to wear hats or veils, fasting and abstinence rules are less rigid. None of these changes, however, will alter the psychological coercion the church continues to inflict by demanding obedience and subservience. Until the church issues a worldwide edict that birth control is okay and convinces Latinas that their bodies are really their own (not their husbands', not the church's or God's), then and only then will the coercion be lessened. Many, many Latinas who were reared under the old regime bear religious scars because they are unable to turn their thinking around.

Furthermore, frequent news stories about the Catholic Church indicate that it is in big trouble—certainly not because I left it, but because *millions* of people, particularly Latinos, are joining other faiths.

Latinoization of the Mormon Church, for example, is rapidly taking place throughout the world. Of five million Mormons world-wide, 17 percent are Latinos. In Mexico, Mormon membership from 1970 to 1980 increased from 75,000 to 276,000. In the United States there are some 200 Mormon churches in Latino communities.

Converts say they are attracted to the Mormon Church by the simplicity of the gospel message and by the social, cultural and educational programs of the church. Yes, Mormons also have many children. The difference is that they believe in education and prosperity; consequently, their quality of life is substantially better.

According to *Nuestro,* a leading Spanish magazine, Latino Mormons may not know their religion thoroughly, but they know its doctrines better than they did their Catholicism. The magazine quotes an elderly Latina who stood up in a Mormon church meeting where church officials were present and said, "I'm grateful to the Virgin of Guadalupe for having brought me to the Mormon Church."

The Mormon Church, however, is not the only one battling for the Latino's heart, mind and soul. The Southern Baptist Convention in Texas calls itself the "largest Spanish-speaking Protestant group in the world," with eighteen hundred churches already functioning and plans for four thousand more. The Apostolic Assembly of the Faith in Jesus Christ in Los Angeles (the city with the largest Latino population outside of Mexico City) boasts fifty-two Spanish congregations, with more being added monthly. The United Methodists also want their share of Latinos and got their first Hispanic bishop in 1985. The same year the East Side Presbyterian Church in Stockton, California, hired a Latino minister to organize Spanish-speaking congregations there.

Exactly what is causing the mass exodus from Catholicism has not been pinpointed by church representatives. My guess is that, since so many Latinos are Catholic in name only, or, if you will, "cultural Catholics," they are prime targets for better offers from other churches. Only 30 percent of Latinos go to mass on Sunday. According to Silvio Cardinal Oddi, "A lot of people don't confess anymore." Catholic services also continue to be boring and nonmotivating. In short, the mass is a downer! Elizabeth, a young Latina, states:

> Within the Catholic Church you're not a person, a human being, an individual—you're only a "child of God." I never felt like an adult, whole, with aspirations when I went to mass. I rarely got something for myself; I only went to give.

In today's stressful world, people need solutions to problems. They want to know how to live better. They want to hear that God loves them. Although non-Catholic churches teach that there is a Supreme Being, they also teach that human beings on Earth are worthy and that God beholds them as creatures deserving of love and success, health and wealth. Why not? If God had not intended for us to have it all, He would not have given us such fantastic minds. He could very well have kept us without the power of thought, like trees or animals.

Gradually losing many of its parishioners, priests and much of its power, the Catholic Church is due for a major overhaul. In the face of adversity, the pyramid of authority is slowly crumbling.

Had the Catholic Church awakened earlier to the real needs of people and the more specific needs of Latinos, it wouldn't be so busy trying to catch up today.

In the *Dictionary of Mexican-American History,* authors Meier and Rivera document the historical unrest among Catholic Mexican Americans.

The Chicano can be seen as a nonparticipant in the official structures of the church and as an object of missionary care. Of fifty-nine thousand American priests today, less than two hundred are Chicanos. Another 385 Hispanic priests have been brought into the United States from Spain or countries other than Mexico. The situation with regard to Hispanic religious sisters and brothers is quite the same.

It was during the late 1960's that Chicanos began to overtly resist their position in the church. From one end of the Southwest to the other, protests and confrontations took place. In San Jose, California, the Chicano Priests' Organization, which had been formed in May of 1969 to provide ministerial and political support to the Chicano movement, picketed the dedication of the multimillion-dollar St. Mary's Cathedral in San Francisco. Many considered this church an extravagant expense in a time of great social need. Near San Diego, Católicos por la Raza occupied church-owned Camp Oliver on November 29, 1969, and demanded a better distribution of church resources for the poor. In Los Angeles, on December 24 of that year another group by the same name demonstrated in front of the new St. Basil's Cathedral. In Las Vegas, New Mexico, Chicanos occupied the vacant Montezuma Seminary on August 26, 1973. In Arizona during most of 1975, a protracted dispute occurred between the Bishop of Phoenix and a coalition of Indians and Chicanos.

Protests also occurred within the national church structure. Early in 1970, Chicano priests formed

PADRES, Padres Asociado para Derecho Educativos y
Sociales, as a vehicle for communication with the bish-
ops. Hispanic nuns formed Las Hermanas, on April 3,
1971.

Meier and Rivera report facts. An unexpected one reveals the
prejudice of the Catholic Church against turn-of-the-century Mexicans. "Here and there, signs appeared in back of Catholic churches
saying LAST THREE ROWS FOR MEXICANS."

Religion for Prosperity

Because I am convinced that the Catholic Church has played a big
role in keeping Latinas down and poor, I want to repeat and stress
that the acceptance of poverty is the worst of our hang-ups.

Earlier I said it takes a lot to beat poverty but mostly it takes
positive mental energy and self-motivation. Well, this is what I
really meant. It takes *courage* and positive mental energy and self-
motivation to:

get an education

take correspondence courses

go to night school

send twenty résumés out every week

beat the pavement and fill out ten job applications per day

tell everyone you know that you're looking for a job and ask
for their help

prepare yourself physically and mentally for successful job interviews

see to your child-care, transportation and wardrobe needs

take an entry-level position for starters but insist on working your way up the ladder

relocate to where the good jobs are

be fiercely determined to improve your lot

Do you see what *courage* can do for you? When you feel low and depressed from living in poverty, you suffer. This suffering is a mental handicap preventing you from going after what you need— more money!

Stop the suffering routine. Just as you've been programmed to accept poverty, you can program yourself to think and accept prosperity and make it your reality. One Latina, Josephine, who spent many years being poor and depressed, says:

I found a new way of thinking. I got more from one reading of *The Power of Positive Thinking* than from all the Hail Marys and Our Fathers I had recited in my lifetime.

Instead of the old prayers, try these Unity Church thoughts that are filled with uplifting hope and a touch of good humor instead of suffocating guilt.

CHRIST IN ME IS THE OPEN DOOR TO NEW IDEAS.
I ENTER A NEW LIFE OF PROSPERITY AND SUCCESS.

There may be several doors that could lead to prosperity and success, but there is one door that I can be sure will open to a new life of greater good for me.

Christ in me is that open door, the door that brings new ideas. These new ideas are divine ideas, which are creative ideas that bring a greater flow of prosperity and success into my life.

If I am seeking employment or more creative work, if I am longing for friends or for a feeling of inner peace, I can achieve my heart's desire as I implement divine ideas in my life.

As I enter the door open to new ideas, I enter a new life of prosperity and success. I am a prosperous, successful person through Christ in me.

BILLFOLD BLESSING

Bless this billfold, Lord I pray,
Replenish it from day to day.
May the bills flow in and out,
Blessing people all about.
Help me earn and wisely spend;
Show me when to buy and lend;
Thank You, God, for bills to pay
For the things I need each day.
When it's empty, put in more
From Thy vast, abundant store.
                                        Amen

Have *courage*, Chiquita! Photocopy "Billfold Blessing" and put it in your wallet.

PART
2

Courage, Chiquita!
The Best Is Yet to Come!

It's Up to Me

Courage to Change

Congratulations! You made it, and the best is yet to come! I know the first seven chapters were tough, but when you think about it, they have given us the opportunity to plunge into the cultural us. And now, within our grasp, is the chance to better ourselves as a result of this learning!

Remember, this book was written to help Latinas who *want* to become aware of cultural confinement and who *want* to change, as well as to help women of other cultures with similar problems.

Think of it this way. An athlete only improves her game after she recognizes and corrects her weaknesses. Successful people succeed because they learn from their failures. Doctors only prescribe after a diagnosis.

Assuming you want to change (otherwise, why would you

have bought this book?), give each of the following statements serious thought.

Change is disruptive.

Change does not occur overnight.

Change requires desire and *courage*.

Change is not easy.

When there is no change, things remain the same.

It's one thing, for example, to want to tell your partner to get his own beer, yet another to be able to handle any possible retaliation. You declare, "I'm not going to mass anymore," but you must prepare yourself to face reactions from family and friends and, very possibly, even your own guilt. Assert yourself when taking steps to reach your goals, but at the same time strive to keep a balance between your goal setting and whatever else is important in your life.

As stated earlier, change can occur in small steps or giant ones. Both work. *You,* however, are the only one who knows which action to take and how much to *risk* at any given time, as well as how much you want to gain. It's essential to think through your actions for change before you attempt them.

In Part II, you'll learn how the mind works and about what I call mindpower philosophies. The purpose of this section is to help you leave the old cultural-cocoon thinking behind and adopt more contemporary views. To try these new philosophies, however, you will need megadoses of courage and desire, which can only come from *within* you. Here's why.

Everything starts from the power of each individual's mind.

This is a basic, universal law. Because this is so, it is important to understand the basic workings of the mind and how it is influenced *before* you attempt any new thinking. This preliminary preparation will help you manage your feelings and any uncertainty or doubt. In the next chapter we'll go into the dynamics of mindpower to show you how to get more out of life, but for now let's tackle how the mind works.

You're reading this book, right? When you want to put it down, the thought crosses your mind. However, it isn't until you actually make the decision to put the book down that your mind will command your hand to carry out the order. This is an oversimplified example, of course, but it illustrates how we do things. At this point, the decision to put the book down is relatively simple.

Taking it a step further, however, even a simple thought process (always starting from within) can become complicated when the dimensions of attitudes, feelings, beliefs, habits and values are added. Suppose, for instance, you start to put the book down. Then you think, "No, I want to see what happens in this chapter." Your belief jumps in and says, "It is not a good idea to quit in the middle of a chapter." Then your value voice chides, "I've got to finish it tonight. I won't have time to read tomorrow." What started out as a *simple* decision gets confusing. As a result, you'll hedge about putting the book down until the strongest influence wins out. Then you'll act accordingly. Recall how many times you have said to yourself, "I sure wish I could make up my mind."

Well, similarly, and as you have already learned, in a specific cultural cocoon, certain learned attitudes, beliefs and values are always jumping in and out of our thought processes. This is much more complicated, because we are now talking about the many influences—family, peer group, religion and culture—that literally put us through distressing paces during our lives. Because these influences automatically enter the decision-making process, making drastic changes or facing new challenges is very tough.

No doubt about it: Thinking a new way is scary. But remember, the life that is a little scary is an exciting and adventurous one. If you never try something new, you may never experience change. You may never progress. Most assuredly, you'll never approach your potential.

Ultimately, what is important is for you to realize that you do have a choice as to how you live your life. You have the option to remain as you are, trapped in a cultural cocoon, or you can *courageously* exercise your right to break free. You can emerge like a butterfly as a free-thinking self-reliant Latina who loves life and who loves being who she is—*al fin, una mujer libre.*

Courage, Chiquita. It's time to be a free woman at last.

Take Charge of Your Life

By now you're surely feeling a surge of energy to make something happen through your own power—so are you ready to drop the old and start the new?

Great! Here's your very first new philosophy:

IT'S UP TO ME.

Repeat: IT'S UP TO ME.

Again: IT'S UP TO ME.

That's it. Drill into your thinking until it becomes second nature: **IT'S UP TO ME. IT'S UP TO ME. IT'S UP TO ME.**

IT'S UP TO ME is the most basic, most valuable self-help theory there is. It can help everyone, everywhere. No matter where you are, whom you are with or what you are doing, when you use these words, you'll find your life functioning in a more positive way and more things going your way.

Before you begin, however, you must come to grips with a very important truth that can really help you once you realize its validity. It may be hard to understand and believe at first, but it is the true wisdom of life. This truth: You are responsible for your own life and happiness. Yes, *you.* Not your mother, father, sisters, brothers, husband, relatives, friends, lover, boyfriends, teachers, government, church or any other person or entity.

Almost everything happening to you is the result of either your *action* or your *inaction.*

Startling? It shouldn't be. It is just a fact of life, which you must face if you are to succeed in getting what you want. It means: "Grow up. Become an adult." Too rough for you? Don't think you can handle it? Sure you can. I know you have the stuff and you'll soon know it too. Otherwise, why would you still be reading? As you continue you'll see how being totally responsible for yourself is an advantage. You'll see that the self-help power resulting from acceptance of the wisdom of this basic law, IT'S UP TO ME, will quickly better your position in almost any situation.

Now you are ready to take charge of your life. Watch out. This is dynamite!

Here's an example. You are out shopping. Your kids are misbehaving and the store clerk has overcharged you on several items. It's been a long day, you're in a hurry to get home to fix a special dinner and you feel that life is treating you unfairly.

STOP! Think for a moment. Life hasn't singled you out to

have a bad day. There's a person who can do something about this situation, and that person is *you!* You're under stress; you must act to alleviate it. IT'S UP TO YOU. Take it a step at a time. Discipline the children firmly, so they know you are in charge. Look at the clerk's name tag, saying, "Oh, Carol, you overcharged me on three items." Smile and ask for a refund. Forget the special dinner you were planning. Choose an easier meal. Better yet, swing by the deli on your way home for some healthy already-cooked entrees. Doing this occasionally won't break your budget. See how IT'S UP TO ME can put control back into your life?

Suppose, however, you don't take any action. The kids will get naughtier, you'll drive home too fast, putting everyone in jeopardy, and cooking your special dinner will seem like twice the work as you continue to fume at the store clerk. Why do this to yourself? Wouldn't it be simpler to outsmart the pressures before they turn into real stress? There is much to be said for facing life's little irritations when they happen.

Here's another example. Suppose you're at a Chinese restaurant with your boyfriend. He orders the usual dinner for two although you had told him earlier you wanted to try something new. Do you assume he has already forgotten what you said? Do you fear he'd think you a nag if you brought it up again? Do you give up with, "Oh, well, maybe next time"? Or do you just feel sorry for yourself and not enjoy the food at all? Do thoughts like these start whirling in your mind, overwhelming you and keeping you from getting what you really want?

STOP!

Remember about your new motto. That's right. IT'S UP TO ME.

You are the one in this situation and *you* can do something about it. It's up to you to go after what you want by reminding yourself of what you planned to have and speaking up to say what you'd like to eat. If you don't use the IT'S UP TO ME approach, for sure you'll be eating what you don't want.

It is interesting to watch people waiting in lines. You hear a lot of grumbling. "What's taking so long?" "My meter is going to run out." "The baby is getting fussy." The complainers psychologically support each other. Yet many people do nothing about the situation. They just accept the status quo without questioning, without realizing that perhaps, just perhaps, they may have some power within themselves to take action.

The IT'S UP TO ME philosophy applies here too. It's up to *you* to find out if you're in the right line. It's up to *you* to ask why the line is moving so slowly. It's up to *you* to refeed the meter or move the car to avoid getting a ticket. It's up to *you* to seek an alternate solution to standing in line. It's up to *you* if you choose to tolerate an intolerable situation.

IT'S UP TO ME is your greatest motivator. Without it, things will always seem to be happening *to* you, instead of *for* you.

As another example, consider your responsibility for yourself in personal relationships. Think of how IT'S UP TO ME could give you the inner courage to get away from undesirable company or the wrong kind of crowd. Think of being in a relationship that might have caused you great unhappiness but leaves you stuck for lack of strength to get out of it. IT'S UP TO ME can help you start anew.

You can also use IT'S UP TO ME on the job, especially in the awesome task of getting a raise. Ever heard of a boss coming up to an employee and saying, "Maria, today I'm going to give you a raise"? Not usually.

If Maria really wants a raise, she must remind herself, "It's up to me. I deserve a raise. I will go after one." It's also up to her to review her position and justify the reasons for her raise. She must believe in herself to be taken seriously and she must be serious about getting the raise. She must risk taking her request to whatever management level is necessary. The same approach would apply to a transfer, promotion or new position. People get what they want when they put themselves in motion and go after it, prepared and with vigor!

Devictimize Yourself

You may be saying, "But it's *not* only up to me. There's everybody else to consider."

No one is telling you to give up your consideration of others but rather *to learn how to take action for yourself in relation to others.* For instance, in line you won't scream at the people; you'll speak politely. At the same time, you can ask for alternate solutions. If you find out the line is delayed due to a shortage of staff, you may choose to return another day. Knowing is much better than waiting for hours, frustrated and irritated. *¿Qué no?* ["No?"]

Using the IT'S UP TO ME philosophy can spur you to the first step of accomplishing something you want or need. Most often, there will still be steps two, three, four or even more. The crucial step is that first one that starts you moving, the one where you choose not to just wait or be victimized. By using IT'S UP TO ME, *you put yourself in motion to get what you want.*

The housewife who decides to go back to school faces a perfect example of a decision that requires more than one step to achieve. She has a husband and three children and isn't sure how she'll be able to combine school and household chores. Once she's made her decision, she needs to inform her family. Ideally, they will work out a plan for managing the household. If she doesn't get their cooperation, she truly knows what she's up against, doesn't she? Whether she returns to school or not will depend on how strong her desire is. In the final analysis, it's still up to her.

The IT'S UP TO ME philosophy sounds tough, because it seems that you're the sole actor. So what? Be *courageous*. Straighten your backbone. Take the risk. IT'S UP TO ME is like being on a diet. No one can lose the weight for you; you have to do it yourself. Just as you have visions of yourself as slim, sexy and stylish, you should have visions of yourself in control of the things you want.

Acting and Reacting

Have you ever been around a group of women who do nothing but whine? They gripe about their husbands, boyfriends, friends, kids, jobs, teachers, cars, prices, clothes, health, money and a hundred other problems. They have so many complaints you wonder what is right in their lives. They complain because they spend most of their lives reacting rather than acting. Someone is always doing something *to* them, making them unhappy. Instead of employing the IT'S UP TO ME view, they merely accept things as they are and store up their grievances until someone listens.

Reacting is letting our actions be determined by other people or events. You are reacting if you think like this: "I'll see what Bob wants to do first, then if there's time I'll do my things." Or, "I think I'll wait for the girls to call before I make any plans." Or, "If Andrea doesn't go shopping with me, I won't go." Reacting is generally that very first emotional action or thought that comes to us when we don't think clearly.

Acting, on the other hand, is deliberate action, putting into effect a determination of our will, making our own independent decision.

Acting is orchestrating, directing and accomplishing things as *you* set out to do. For example, "Bob, let's coordinate our schedules so we can both get something done." Or, "My plans are set; I'll share them with the girls when they call." Or, "I can go shopping by myself if Andrea doesn't want to go."

And as for that chronic complainer, the best way to handle her is to say, "Well, what are you doing about it?"

All of you are victims of habits, but being a reactor is one of the worst ones because you allow everyone else in your life to call the shots. Maybe you have other limitations you feel you can't overcome and so you wish a lot . . . I wish I could stop smoking . . . I wish I were more energetic . . . I wish I weren't such a worrier . . .

STOP!

Just wishing is fruitless. You're the one with the behavior that makes you unhappy. It is your responsibility to do something about it.

Many people say, "I can't" when they really mean, "I don't" or "I won't."

To break any unwanted habit, you must put yourself in the IT'S UP TO ME mode. Sometimes you may choose to ask for support or help. For example, you may not be able to stop smoking alone, so you seek help from a program or some counseling. Blessedly, we live in a free-advice world. No matter what problem we need to tackle, there's lots of free information available. Still, it's up to you to tap the resources you need.

There are many wonderful things about IT'S UP TO ME. It's free. It's available to everyone. It has no age or sex limits. *And* it's controlled by you. When you start to use it, the results are amazing.

Si Dios Quiere—
A Loser's Philosophy

In using the IT'S UP TO ME philosophy you may experience some conflict with the old cultural philosophy of *si Dios quiere* ["if God wills it"]. If you were reared hearing "si Dios quiere" over and over, you are probably programmed to wait for things to happen, as opposed to making them happen. To one degree or another, we are all programmed with messages. Some tend to affect us more deeply than others, just as some people are more affected than others.

Be aware. You have probably heard "si Dios quiere" zillions of times, witnessed it in operation and still not realized its effect upon your behavior.

"Si Dios quiere" is somewhat similar to *"que será, será,"* but it is much more serious because of its religious basis. These messages reinforce indecisiveness, pessimism and even go to the extreme of "I can't plan anything for next week. I might not even be alive!" This is total negative thinking! These kinds of thoughts can prevent you from ever reaching your goals!

During my childhood, I wanted to scream every time I heard my mother say, "Si Dios quiere." No matter what the issue at hand, it was her automatic response. I often wondered what God knew about my getting new shoes or the family's going to the Cinco de Mayo fiesta. If mamá didn't already know, how and when was God going to give her the answer?

My mother, of course, was not alone in using this famous slogan. Everybody used it. Telephone conversations always ended, "I'll call you again next week," to which the other replied, "Sí, si Dios quiere." When company left, "Well, good-bye. We'll see you at mass on Sunday." "Sí, si Dios quiere." Crimeneeeeeeee! Didn't *anyone* have any confidence in ideas, in planning, in faith, in tomorrow, in themselves?

I don't think "si Dios quiere" has anything to do with God's wanting us to do or not to do something. Nor does He expect us to wait for His guiding light or green signal for everyday activities. He gave us all good minds with which to make decisions but we forgot how to use them. As a consequence, we began to rely heavily on Him to show us the way.

The sad part of using "si Dios quiere" as a philosophy for living is that it becomes an alibi, an excuse and a crutch for inaction. It suggests that you wait, when perhaps you should be moving. It triggers a red light, not a green one. For me, it constituted a "What's the use" attitude. It gave me the feeling that nothing better was going to happen tomorrow because nothing was or could be planned ahead. This isn't living; it is existing. It is acceptance of whatever comes our way with no thought of taking charge of our situations, no hope for fuller lives.

"Si Dios quiere" is a loser's philosophy. Bury it! Refuse to let it pass your lips! Take the talent and *mind* and ambitions God gave you and use them freely. He wants you to make good use of them.

Why else would He have given them to you! It's not up to God, believe me; it's up to *you*!

Bingo!

No matter who you are, where you come from, with whom you share your life, what you're doing or where you're headed, your life is based on your own individual action or inaction.

So think. Make decisions. Take action. Then you'll get results. IT'S UP TO ME is a crucial concept. Today, in your life, plant the seed: IT'S UP TO ME

> when I want a new dress.
>
> when I want a better car.
>
> when I want a new house.
>
> when I want a boyfriend who treats me like a queen.
>
> when I want respectable friends.
>
> when I want a better-paying job.
>
> when I want to finish my education.
>
> when I want to move to Hawaii.
>
> when I want to become an actress.
>
> when I want to be slim and sexy.
>
> when I want private schools for my children.
>
> when I want a more loving husband.

Now add your own IT'S UP TO ME

when I _____.
when I _____.
when I _____.

When I want a happy and fulfilling life:

IT'S UP TO ME!

MOTIVATING MESSAGE

CHIQUITA'S OLD CULTURE   CHIQUITA'S NEW COURAGE

SI DIOS QUIERE.   IT'S UP TO ME!

["IF GOD WILLS IT."]

Mindpower

*L*uis Valdez, political activist, famous playwright and director of
Zoot Suit and *La Bamba,* graciously gave away his secret of success
in a television interview. When asked what had made him successful, he pointed to his head and said, "It's all up here. It's all in
believing in what you are doing and in putting your mind to getting
it done."

Luis Valdez meant every word literally. He spends a "quiet
time" each day by himself, with himself. Before he begins his day,
Luis politely says, "Excuse me, I have to go do my thing." "His
thing" means finding a quiet place where he can have a private
dialogue with each thought going on in his mind. With intense
concentration, he orders his mindpower to turn his visions—his
creative ideas, his organization's administrative needs and his family's needs—into reality. He concentrates with extra punch on his
relentless search for solutions to the many problems affecting Latinos, especially farmworkers. A firm believer in "doing his thing,"

Luis has a special room in his home that is used only for this purpose. It is empty, undecorated and locks from the inside. "The fewer distractions, the easier my concentration, the better my mindpower responds," declares Luis.

Like Luis Valdez, each of us possesses potentially fantastic mindpower. When we learn how to develop and use it—it's *La Bamba* time!

So jump into this chapter with both feet. Get excited about the dynamics of mindpower and learn more about how *you* can put your mind to work on *your* behalf!

Read, apply, practice. Be like Luis Valdez.

What Is Mindpower?

Mindpower is characterized by various concepts such as picturing/imagining/visualizing, self-talk, positive thinking and positive language usage and like attracts like. These ideas may be unfamiliar to you, but I'll explain them as we go along. There are some questions after each discussion. Take time to understand them and reflect on your answers. The better you see and know your needs, the sooner you can begin to apply the mindpower dynamics and reap the benefits.

As you already know, all things start in the mind with thoughts. Thoughts then lead to decisions. Decisions lead to actions and actions lead to results.

Thoughts

↓

Decisions

↓

Actions

↓

Results

We talk, cry, laugh, walk, sit, stand, run, jump, play or work only after the thought and the decision to do so are completed in our minds. We find jobs, get married, have children, go to college, visit friends, take vacations, attend church or go shopping only because the mind motivates us.

Our minds command our bodies, actions, emotions—in short, our lives. Some functions like breathing and digestion are involuntary; that is, they happen without thought, even if we are unconscious. Others are reflexive, like snatching our fingers away from a hot stove. However, everything else we do, everything we are, is connected with the thoughts in our minds. Our entire lives—whether we live in shacks or mansions, happily or unhappily, in the old ways or in contemporary lifestyles—all stem from the ideas embedded in our minds.

Developing Your Mindpower Through Pictures

Let's go even further. Scientists tell us that we use only 10 percent of our minds. Imagine what we could do if we used the other 90 percent! They also tell us that we don't think in words or thoughts per se, but in pictures. Imagine, *pictures*! For example, let's say you want a new dress. As soon as you create the idea of having a new dress in your mind, you start picturing the style, the material, the color, the fit and even the price range. You shop and shop until you find the dress that matches the picture in your mind. This is how we fulfill our desires, whether it is a new dress, a new car, a new man or a new life. We all shop with preconceived ideas.

Many mindpower experts declare that the act of forming these mental images for our desires is the seed that brings forth our reality. Picturing, imagining and visualizing all mean the same thing; that is, the forming of pictures in our mind. I recommend the books *Magic of Believing* and *TNT: The Power Within You* by Claude Bristol for more study.

Here we go with some questions.

What kind of life, if any, have you pictured for yourself? Did you know you could picture your life?

Now, hang on, here comes the real mind-blower! It has been said over and over that whatever you repeatedly picture in your mind with strong conviction and energy eventually becomes a reality. Let me repeat that. Whatever you repeatedly picture in your mind with strong conviction and energy eventually becomes a reality! This is so significant, I'm going to say it a third time. Whatever you repeatedly picture in your mind with strong conviction and energy eventually becomes a reality!

Magic, you say? Absolutely. It's a good and powerful magic and *you* have it within *you*!

Think for a moment. How many things have been invented because someone pictured an idea? Well, one example is the sewing machine, which was devised because a man pictured a machine that could sew. Think of all the fabulous inventions produced because people had pictures in their heads.

Look around the room you're sitting in. The furniture, the electric light, even the clothes you're wearing were all at one time merely someone's idea. Think of the extraordinary inventions we've had in this century alone: the automobile, automation, space rockets, computers, laser surgery! All of these great ideas and things came from one place and one place only—from the minds of the people who held the picture of them, persisted in their picturing and took action to make their dreams come true.

Another important question to ask yourself is, Are you persistent in the pictures you hold for yourself?

Think of the mind as a garden. When you plant good things, good things will grow, but if you don't plant anything, weeds take over. Or think of the mind as a computer: the better the programming, the better the results. *What you want to do is use your mindpower to get what you want out of life!*

Mindpicturing can change your life to what you want it to be. Remember when you pictured or dreamed of something happening and the dream came true? When this happens, many people tend to consider it mere coincidence, but I'm convinced that it is often a result of your thinking. You can cause something to happen because your mindpower is strong. The power of the mind to make things happen is awesome.

Just as your mind can initiate a "coincidence," you can make things happen by planning them. Remember, *everything* originates in the mind. The biblical passages "For whatever a man soweth, that shall he also reap" and "As a woman thinketh, so shall it be" affirm how the thoughts and pictures we hold in our minds affect our reality.

As a Woman Thinketh
in Matters of the Heart

You can use your mindpower to bring good or ill. Or you can neglect to use it and merely let things happen. IT'S UP TO YOU. Have you ever thought about how you use your thoughts or mindpower in a romantic situation?

Let's say you have a wonderful relationship with Tim. Suddenly he calls it off. You're devastated. You miss him desperately. More than anything, you want him back. You *tell yourself* you're in agony. You *tell yourself* over and over you can't live without him. You spend lonely, sleepless nights and bleak days barely functioning without him. After six months, nine months, a year of this *self-torture,* you begin to wonder why you can't get over him.

Mujeres, the reality is that thoughts cause feelings, not the other way around. This is a very important truth. Thoughts cause feelings but feelings *don't* cause thoughts. For months *you've* fed your mind romantic miseries and that is exactly why you're feeling miserable. As a woman *thinketh,* so shall it *be.* The thoughts you harbor in your mind control you and your feelings.

Yes, the loss of a loved one is very painful. But you can conquer your pain by changing your thinking. Use your dynamic mindpower and reprogram. Repeat to yourself, "I love you, Tim. I forgive you, Tim. I release you, Tim." Let go, and the pain will also go. Yes, you'll still cry, feel blue and perhaps even hate the world; but if you don't let go, you may also make yourself ill and things will only get worse. So feel sad feelings when you have to.

your mindpower to picture yourself free you can be. It is exactly when life throws that we need all the mindpower we can s is hell. But life is a series of endings and

re you using your mindpower to work for

Programming with Positive Self-talk

e babble in your head caused a lot of your in our heads much of the time. Babble is or the "little voice" inside ourselves. We ourselves—about how we feel, what to inner, whether to go out or stay home, to how to pay the bills and, of course, does he or doesn't he love me.

Ever stop to figure out what kind of conversations you hold with yourself? The very best are helpful conversations, full of meaning. Any other kind is negative programming. When you're feeling temporarily low or depressed, is your self-talk "I'm depressed; I'm *so* depressed"? STOP! This is negative programming and all it does is reinforce your depression. Immediately change your self-talk to positive programming: "I'm happy. I'm happy. I'm happy." Keep saying it over and over. If you have to, go somewhere where you can shout "I'M HAPPY!" one hundred times. But whatever you do, don't let the "I'm depressed" guy back in.

A short case of the blues and blahs is one thing. If your depression lingers for more than six weeks you may have what Dr. Nancy C. Andreason calls a "broken brain" and need medical attention. Get it.

If you're in the throes of a problem, don't concentrate on the problem but on the solution. Ask your mindpower for a solution by saying, "I need a solution to . . ." "I need a solution to . . ." Repeat and repeat the "I need a solution" part and the solution will come. This may be very difficult to believe but do it anyway. After it has worked for you once and then twice, it will become easier and easier to believe in your own power.

Just as it is important to listen and improve the kind of conversations you carry on with yourself, it is equally important to scrutinize the kinds of words you use—because the very words you use affect your mindpower. Suppose you constantly say to yourself, "I'm fat." The mind absorbs this message and when it has been repeated enough times will act on it. You will be fat because you programmed your mind to believe that is what you want. Your mind, in turn, commands your body to be fat. Here is more disastrous self-talk:

I don't feel good.

I'm always tired.

I don't have time.

It's impossible.

I don't care.

I'm so dumb.

The more we say these things, the more we act them out. *Everything we say to ourselves, when repeated enough times, sooner or later materializes!*

Watch not only your self-talk but also the language you use with others, because language affects us all profoundly.

When we give a compliment to someone, for example, that person lights up like a Christmas tree:

Gee, Sharon, you look terrific today.

Your garden is just beautiful.

What a great job you did on that report.

Conversely, the language sometimes used in rearing children has a very negative effect:

You don't do well in school because you're lazy.

Clumsy girl, you spilled the milk.

You can't find your shoe because you're so messy.

Turn these around into positive language:

Remember when you're in school today, you are a brilliant and beautiful girl.

Whoops! An accident. You wipe up the milk. I'll refill your glass.

You have such sharp eyes, you'll find your shoe.

We should all bear in mind the adage "If you can't say something nice, don't say anything at all." All language is a form of mental suggestion or mental influence and affects what and how we are. So watch what you say!

What you think shows. Your thoughts affect your posture, facial expression and total body language. People with scowls on their faces are scowling inside. Smiling people have happy thoughts. People who walk tall are energetic in their thoughts. Your character and personality come from the very thoughts you hold.

Do a mirror test whenever you pass one or another reflecting surface. Answer this for yourself: What do your facial expressions and body language say about *your* thoughts?

The Miracle of Like Attracts Like

You've heard the phrase "like attracts like." This is another phenomenon of mindpower. It simply means that you attract what you think. You found that dress you had pictured because you had a "like" image of it in your mind. You can use the power of like attracts like to acquire whatever else you want to bring into your world, be it a new house, a new friend or even money.

My best like-attracts-like program is the one I use to get money. I learned it from the book *The Magic of Believing*. All I do is draw dollar signs over and over. Whenever I'm on the telephone, I doodle dollar signs like this:

$$\$$$
$$\$$$

After I have covered one side of the paper, I turn it over and cover the other side, then start on another piece of paper. I draw fat ones and skinny ones. I go over and over the ones already drawn. I draw dollar signs every chance I get. This may sound crazy, but it works. Through the phenomenon of like attracts like, money comes to me in a variety of ways: a friend paying off an old loan, a rebate I sent in months earlier, payment for an article, selling something I no longer need, a writing commission, more money in my account than I thought I had, a couple of twenties hidden away for a rainy day. It is difficult to explain, but the money does come, just when I need it the most.

You can do this too. Write dollar signs every chance you get and money will come to you. You must, however, firmly believe in this phenomenon, you must have a burning desire to make it happen and you must be persistent. Let's remind ourselves that poverty is pain and while money is not an end in itself, it does provide your family's needs and we need to get more of it.

How about a boyfriend? Would you like to bring the right man into your life? You can, you know. Picture in your mind the way you want him to look, his personality, his voice quality, his status and even the kind of car he drives. When you make the picture clear in your mind and hold it persistently, the magnetism of like attracts like will produce a like image. Such a person will enter your life.

The same holds true for a new house. If you want one, picture exactly what you want. Put the positive images into play. Don't worry about the details, such as how you're going to pay for it. That will take care of itself. Fervently, start picturing yourself living in your dream house.

Now you must really think I'm crazy. Nope. Just a believer.

When you were a little girl, didn't you dream of your Prince Charming? Didn't you dream of the little house with the white picket fence? Marriage? Having babies? Did your dreams come true? I'll bet that some of them did.

As Latinas we have seen firsthand the results of failure to use mindpower to our people's advantage. Latinos, we know, are hard-working people. No matter what our country of origin, we all possess a single-minded plan of working in order to sustain ourselves and our families.

Unfortunately, this is where we have failed, because hard work is not enough. Hard work doesn't guarantee success. Many people work hard all of their lives and have very little to show for it.

As a child picking grapes, I saw that although we worked hard, we never really got anywhere. Finishing one crop meant starting another. We were so busy working hard, bent and stooped over, it never occurred to us to stand up straight and look around for better opportunities. By settling for the first job we found, we eliminated any chance for better ones. Had we used our minds more and our backs less, we would have had many more opportunities available to us. *¡Qué lástima!* ["What a pity."]

I was fortunate. I used my hot years under the grapevines to dream and picture. My self-talk went like this: "I hate the heat and this dirty work. When I get older I'm going to work in an air-conditioned office and live in a big, cool house. I'm going to go to school and study so I won't have to work in the fields all my life. I'm going to marry a kind, generous man. He'll be an elegant dresser and have a briefcase."

Would you believe I married exactly such a man, who later became an attorney and turned out to be a clotheshorse. We get what we picture. Throughout my life, the many pictures I have held steady in my mind have materialized. They can and will for you too.

"A man's thoughts make him or break him" is a truism. It's the power of thought that brings about success, wealth and material gain. Creative thinking is the tool you need for a life above poverty. Believing in yourself and having persistent faith can bring you a better life.

Mindpower for Healing

Before we get you started using your mindpower for the things you want in life, there's one last miracle of the mind I want to share with you—the mind's power to heal. Stories of successful mind healing come out every day, some so dramatic and incredible that they are beyond the comprehension of the medical profession. Most of these healings are based on the use of powerful thoughts like "I made up my mind to get well," "I saw myself walking again," "I knew I had to change my negative attitude to a positive one." There are more and more clinics that teach positive mental programming and visualization techniques as treatment (in conjunction with conventional medical care) for even the worst diseases. Next time you start to say "I don't feel good," STOP! Say instead, "I feel fine," "I'm healthy," "I am healthy now and forever." Repeat it and mean it!

All of this is *extremely* important, especially since studies in the *Journal of the American Medical Association* have found that Latinos have longer and more expensive hospital stays than whites.

Let's think seriously about this one. What health self-messages do you live by?

Now focus on all these mindpower concepts together—picturing/imagining/visualizing, self-talk, positive thinking and positive language usage and like attracts like. What exactly is the overall message? Simply this: *Turn your thoughts into achievements.*

There are many books on the power of the mind. Read some of them. None of these ideas is new. The one that is most comfortable for you is the one you should use. But believe that mindpower is indeed all powerful.

You Want It, You Got It!

Okay. Let's get you started. Grab some paper and a pencil. List all the things you want. Don't be scared or shy or feel that you might seem greedy. Just do it. List everything—ten or one hundred items, small or large, tangible or intangible, for tomorrow or for years in the future, for yourself or for your family. List, list, list!

Why the lists? Because knowing what you want is the first step to achievement. The second step is to have a burning desire to achieve. The third, a plan of action. And fourth, to persist.

Go back over your list and put a big star by the entries for which you have a burning desire. Write each of these on a separate 3" × 5" index card, using the five Ws—who, what, when, where and why as a guide to cover all bases.

> *Example:* I, Maria Delores, am a med student at UCLA
> by _____ (*date*). I see myself with all the financial aid
> I need. I see myself successfully adapting to the educa-
> tion process and college life. I graduate in _____ (*date*).

Repeat and visualize, repeat and visualize.

> *Example:* My family has a new home on 1234 Drive, Anywhere, USA, by _____ (*date*). We enjoy four large bedrooms, three bathrooms, an extra game room, a spacious family room, a laundry room and a warm party-size kitchen. The yard is a perfect size with flourishing fruit trees and flowers and a working garage. The neighborhood is safe, clean and friendly. The nearby schools are caring. The Sanchez family has a new home, the Sanchez family has a new home, the Sanchez . . .

Repeat and visualize, repeat and visualize.

> *Example:* The perfect job is waiting for me by _____ (*date*). I am the supervisor of XYZ's Customer Service Department.

Repeat and visualize, repeat and visualize.

Write specifics on each card. Include as much concrete information as possible.

These are now your affirmation cards. The word "affirmation" means "to make firm." You are going to use your cards to fix, or make firm, the picture of what you want in your mind. Read the cards and visualize the pictures over and over again throughout the day. To speed up the process, make several sets of cards, wrap each set with a rubber band and place them where they will be readily available. For example, I carry some in my purse. I use this set the most, especially when I'm waiting in lines. I have another set on my nightstand to read and picture just before going to sleep. I also have a set taped around my makeup mirror to review each morning.

Affirmation cards are powerful tools with which to program your mind for what you want out of life. You can hold only one thought in mind at a time; therefore, these affirmations keep you on track and eliminate the useless babble that might otherwise monopolize your thoughts. Once you've become experienced in using affirmation cards, you'll find you won't need to write down your goals. You'll simply create new ones and recite them automatically. Whenever you wish to, you can change your affirmations.

Always keep your mind affirming for the things you desire. When you're not affirming a specific goal, affirm a general one, such as: "Every day, in every way, my life is better."

I like this particular affirmation because I can change the ending to exactly what I need:

"Every day, in every way, I'm healthier."
"Every day, in every way, I'm richer."
"Every day, in every way, I'm a better writer."
"Every day, in every way, I'm a better mother."
"Every day, in every way, I'm a better listener."
"Every day, in every way, _____."
"Every day, in every way, _____."
"Every day, in every way, _____."

Or you can combine them dynamically:

"Every day, in every way, my life is better in work, love, play, health, finances, parenting."

Fiesta time for this one!

The more specific the affirmation, the stronger the force of attraction. As you read and recite your affirmations, visualize your goals as though they have already happened. This creates dual power. Remember: To make the affirmation stick, you must repeat, repeat, repeat without letup.

Your affirmations become a reality faster when you start a plan of action. Remember the line in the previous chapter, "Put yourself in motion"? On the back of your affirmation cards, jot down the things you must do to make your dreams come true. Then do them.

Maria Delores: Get, fill out and submit application to UCLA.

Sanchez family: Call a real estate agent. Start looking.

XYZ supervisor: Apply for the position. Start politics.

Remember, you want it, you got it!

Affirmations Are Dynamite!

I began to use written affirmations when I decided I wanted to become a writer. In fact, it was my writing professor who said, "If you are going to be a writer, you must first truly believe that you can become one." He told us to write and recite: "I'm a writer. I'm a writer. I'm a writer." Then he said to change to: "I'm a published writer. I'm a published writer." I did. Then I took the next step: "I'm a successful writer. I'm a successful writer. I'm a successful writer." This indeed worked. I sold everything I wrote! Apparently, it also worked for his eighteen hundred other students, who, together over a period of ten years, have sold more than a total of $1 million worth of articles and books!

My winning a BMW is a more incredible example of how powerful affirmations can be. To all you skeptics out there—every detail of this story is true.

At the college where I worked, hundred-dollar raffle tickets for a brand-new BMW were being sold. With no spare hundred dollars, I organized a pool of ten people to buy a ticket jointly and I typed ten affirmation cards, one for each person in the pool. They read:

> I [*individual name*] have won the 1983 BMW raffle on
> Sunday, 11/27/83, by American River College in Sac-
> ramento, California.

I instructed each person to repeat the affirmation frequently and to keep the card where it would be seen often until the day of the drawing. Because I was going out of town, I taped mine to the dashboard of my car and read it over and over while en route. Our ticket was the winner!

Do I truly believe that these affirmation cards helped us win the car? Absolutely! All the people in my pool were strong mind-power believers. I sincerely believe that our combined mental energy won that car for us!

One last suggestion and then you're on your way. Write yourself a fifteen-second commercial. A commercial? Yes, like this one:

Maria! Meet Maria—an important, really important person. Maria, you're a big thinker, so *think big* about everything. You've got plenty of ability to do a first-class job, so do a first-class job. Be a prosperous woman. You can be. You have lots of energy, Maria, lots of energy. Put it to work. Nothing can stop you. You look good, Maria, and you feel good. You're in perfect health mentally, emotionally, physically and spiritually. Stay this way. Look sharp and be sharp. Think big about *everything*. Anything you want can be yours. *Anything*. Belief magnetizes. Money likes being in your purse. Money belongs in your purse.

Program yourself with your commercial, just as other commercials do, using repetition. Be sure to use your commercial when you're having a bad day. Use it to keep yourself up and moving, to remind yourself what a great person you are and can be.

Start your affirmations and self-reformation today. You can have what you want and need in life if you can just remember to use your mindpower. Your mind is your higher power.

Chiquita, I'm going to close this chapter with a wonderful excerpt from *The Dynamic Laws of Prosperity,* a book by Catherine Ponders, who wants you to say to yourself:

> I am an irresistible magnet, with the power to attract
> unto myself everything that I divinely desire, according
> to the thoughts, feelings and mental pictures I constantly
> entertain and radiate. I am the center of my universe! I
> have the power to create whatever I wish. I attract what-

ever I mentally choose and accept. I begin choosing and mentally accepting the highest and best in life. I now choose and accept health, success and happiness. I now choose lavish abundance for myself and for all mankind. This is a rich, friendly universe and I dare to accept its riches, its hospitality and to enjoy them now!

MOTIVATING MESSAGE

CHIQUITA'S OLD CULTURE   CHIQUITA'S NEW COURAGE

VAMOS A VER.   I *CAN* MAKE IT HAPPEN.
["WE SHALL SEE."]

10

Asking and Risking

*A*s parents, we spend years counseling our children both informally—by nagging and scolding—and formally—with explanations and discussions. We teach morals, good manners, cleanliness, studying and working hard. But above all, we yearn to give our offspring that one piece of advice, that one special message that will help them succeed in life.

The message I preached to my offspring at least a million times is ASK. To get what you want out of life you must learn to ask. And asking means you must take a risk. Maybe I said it two million times because the risking part posed such a threat. The sermons took years but were worth it.

My fourteen-year-old daughter, Stacey, who was accustomed to receiving jewelry whenever her father returned from an out-of-town business trip, one day asked me to ask him not to bring her any more earrings. She wanted necklaces or bracelets instead.

"Fine," I said. "When Dad comes home, *ask* him for that. It's up to you, not me, to let him know what you want."

When Stacey turned eighteen, she chose a local seafood restaurant for her big night out, but when we got there she was unhappy with her food and said we should have gone to San Francisco for real lobster. "Well, Stacey," I replied, "we could have, but you didn't *ask* to go to San Francisco."

Adult Stacey, catching on and braving the risk of *asking,* one day surprised me by saying she was going to *ask* for a hundred-dollar raise. When I inquired if that was what she really wanted she replied that she really needed three hundred dollars. Looking her straight in the eye, I said, "Then why not *ask* for three hundred dollars?" Stacey asked for three hundred dollars and got two hundred fifty dollars.

Overcoming the Fear of Asking and Risking

There are many kinds of risks—foolish risks, small risks and big risks. The speeding idiot who insists on passing everyone on the freeway takes a foolish risk. A small risk might be returning a dress without the receipt and hoping to get your cash back or asking your boss for a day off during the busy season. Big risks are those milestones we take in our lives—falling in love, marrying, moving and spending sizable amounts of money. In a sense, we are generally better prepared for the big risks because we plan and grow into them naturally in the course of life.

I want to talk about the small, everyday risks that we as Latinas should take more often. Usually we don't take enough risks and, consequently, don't get very far or accomplish much. In general, Latinas are *very* shy when it comes to asking and risking. I believe this is because we've never been taught to ask for the things we need and want. Our cultural programming, our humbling religion and our domination by men have prevented us from being assertive. This may be why we don't do well in school, either. We're afraid to risk asking the teacher for help. Too often we shy away from the mainstream because of limited English and lack of mainstream skills. We settle for the lower-paying jobs because, although we have the intellect and skills for the better ones, we are too shy and scared to ask for or risk more. Because we won't ask and risk, we fail to assert ourselves in a world we expect to be perfect but which is instead full of racism, competition and fast-paced progress. Then we turn around, blame the world for our own shortcomings and murmur, "Poor me."

The basic reason people do not ask for something is that in their minds they are already convinced the answer will be no. Without taking even a casual chance, they bury themselves with negative thinking. How many times have you hesitated about doing something because you thought something bad might happen? Do these sound familiar?

I'd better not go.

I know they'll say no.

What if it rains?

What if it's too crowded?

What if the kids need me?

What if Alex gets upset?

Most of the time fears do not materialize, yet they stop us in our tracks! Fear of the unknown holds us back from asking, risking, doing. Wouldn't life be sweet if we knew everything that was coming our way each day, each hour? Well, we don't and we never will. Overcoming fear of the unknown is imperative!

Tell Your Old Man to Get His Own Beer

Risking means taking the chance to declare what you want—be it a new dress, a new job, asking your children to do for themselves, asking your old man to get his own beer or just letting people know how you honestly feel about certain things. If your life is ever going to change for the better you'll have to take chances. To get out of your cocoon, you will have to meet new people and explore new ideas. You will have to go to unfamiliar places where the language and culture may be different and where you will have to learn your way around on your own.

Walk Tall!

Since nothing is more difficult than putting yourself on the line, taking a risk requires an IT'S UP TO ME attitude. Give yourself a good pep talk, take some very deep breaths and summon up a lot of *courage* to overcome butterflies or knots in your stomach, cold feet, sweaty palms, terror or even nausea. A person who overcomes the anxiety of asking and risking is emotionally mature, secure and confident. A person who risks asking for what he or she wants is alive; the one who doesn't is practically dead.

Day-by-day acts of asking and risking are important because they affect your self-esteem. When you pose a "Should I or shouldn't I?" question to yourself, your subconscious automatically imposes value judgments. "Am I good enough?" you wonder. If you think little of yourself, you won't ask or risk, and the more you think this way the lower your feeling of self-worth goes. This *must* (and can) change. The more often you ask and risk, the more often you succeed and the easier it gets. As a consequence, your self-esteem soars.

For Latinas, the fear of asking and risking in the greater society has much to do with anticipation that the ax of racism will fall. One sees this often in the Latina's hesitation at acting fully on her own behalf in public, whether at restaurants, banks, drugstores, gas stations, shopping malls, schools, job interviews or garage sales. Nothing makes me angrier than to observe this hesitation and see the Latina go away emptyhanded! How can you spot her hesitation? Easy. The soft, nonassertive voice, the backing-off body language, the they-don't-like-us-here facial expression and, finally, her failure.

Much more enraging is the Gothic kind of thinking shown by Roberta, thirty-one, who speaks for all too many Latinas when she admits:

> I don't know why, but every time I go into a business place, everyone is against me. I know it's just because I'm Mexican. This happens to me everywhere.

These are ugly, self-defeating feelings. Harboring and nurturing the thought that the world is conspiring to persecute you because you're Mexican is the Chiquita's cocoon in you! You learned this inferiority complex and you allow it to dominate you only to your own detriment, not anyone else's!

It's doubtful that the whole world is against you because you are Mexican. It is even more doubtful that the world even cares what race you are. However, if you go around with a beaten, hang-dog look as if to say, "I'm Mexican, hurt me," you're bound to get condescension and abuse. Remember the lessons on self-talk and be careful what you tell yourself.

The fact that Roberta and her *amigas* ["girlfriends"] are treated as they are is not because they are Mexican but because of their attitudes. Furthermore, they excuse their failures to justify their actions. What it all boils down to is an unwillingness to take a risk. Using Mexicanness or Latinaness to avoid asking and risking is a loser's way of living.

You're Worth It

Listen!—when you go anywhere, for any kind of service, expect to get it! Approach people politely with the attitude that you are a woman with a mission. Take the risk! Be assertive! Speak up! If indeed you feel negative vibrations, show that in spite of racism or a cold attitude you expect to get what you want. If you are still dissatisfied, *ask* and *risk* more. Question. Probe. Push. Demand. A good tactic is to act like a five-hundred-pound marshmallow taking up all of their time if they don't give you satisfactory service. If politeness fails, be pushy and demanding. Personally, I would rather someone called me a bitch than a dumb Mexican! *Ask* and *risk*. I will. You must too.

MOTIVATING MESSAGE

CHIQUITA'S OLD CULTURE   CHIQUITA'S NEW COURAGE

TENGO MIEDO.   *¡VALENTIA!*

["I'M AFRAID."]   ["BE BRAVE!"]

DO IT! ASK! ASK! ASK!

11

Win at Love, Life, Work and Play by Planning

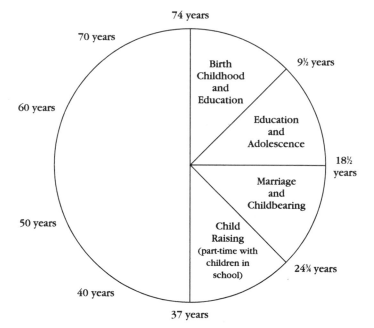

A WOMAN'S LIFE

74 years

70 years

9½ years

60 years

Birth
Childhood
and
Education

Education
and
Adolescence

18½
years

50 years

Marriage
and
Childbearing

Child
Raising
(part-time with
children in
school)

24¾ years

40 years

37 years

This is it! A lifetime right before your very eyes! Women today have a life expectancy of seventy-four years that is *rapidly* increasing to ninety-two years, according to a recent study. Imagine living ninety-two years! *¡Chihuahua!* ["Wow!"] That's a very long time, a long time in which to do many, many things. *¿Sí? ¡Sí!* And here's another fact: Women *outlive* men by more than ten years.

But notice that only the right side of the circle is filled with activity. The left side is blank. *Nada.* Why is this? Do women stop living at thirty-seven, the half-circle mark on the chart? Some do. For example, what happens to a woman who hasn't worked in twenty years if she is suddenly divorced or widowed at age thirty-seven? I will *never* forget my own mother's struggle when she was widowed at thirty-three with seven kids and two bucks.

On the other hand, women who plan ahead find this second half of their lives filled with employment, political activity, community service, church or club work. The circle representing the life cycle points out some important facts for all of us. Young women in the adolescence/education stage should foresee what lies ahead and plan judiciously. The full-time homemaker's child-raising years should also include time to continue her education or work in preparation for the last half of her life. We must stop, mark the spot where we are now and think seriously about what lies ahead. Although we can't change the past, we can certainly identify the stage where we are now and plan a new and better future.

That circle presents only one way of looking at the scheme or design of life. Here are four other interpretations.

1. Youth—Middle Age—Golden Years

2. Learning—Working—Playing

3. Education—Work—Family—Retirement

4. Infancy—Early Childhood—Play Age—School Age—
    Adolescence — Young Adulthood — Adulthood — Old
    Age

Sociologists predict our lifetime behavior:

16–18 Time to break away from our parents.

19–22 Still trying to get away. Friends become our allies
    until they leave home. When their once-cherished
    loyalty is gone, we're forced to find our own paths.

23–28 A time of experimentation and growth. The feeling
    that everything will work out. It is "all within my
    control." An optimistic stage.

29–33 The pleasures and fun of the earlier phases tire us.
    More serious questions arise: "Am I doing what I'm
    really supposed to be doing with my life?"

34–43 Feelings of nervousness about how we've spent our
    first thirty-three years of life. Worry over the present
    and the future. "Is there time to change?" Our chil-
    dren reach independence and our aging parents de-
    mand more attention. We look to our spouses for
    more understanding, but they look for the same sup-
    port.

44–53 Stability sets in. Mortality becomes real. Spouses are
    reunited in companionship. "Here I am. I can deal
    with life."

54–on A period of mellowing and warming up to self, parents and friends. Careers end. Retirement. Depending on health and energy, there are new careers, part-time employment, continuing education, hobbies, travel.

Human Needs and Life Planning with Señor Maslow

Understanding life-planning models is important because they help us see ahead. They are the foundation upon which we build. However, in order for our life cycles to be complete, and to survive happily, we must nourish many needs.

Food We must eat to live.

Housing We need shelter.

Love Love is most essential.

Faith We need to have spiritual belief outside ourselves.

To belong Belonging gives us a sense of identity.

A sense of accomplishment We need to fulfill a purpose.

Recognition We need to have recognition from others.

Health We need to be healthy.

Security We need to feel secure.

Being creative We want to express our creativity.

Self-improvement We want to improve ourselves.

Money We're entitled to enjoy the fruits of our labor, buying pleasures as well as necessities.

The prominent psychologist Abraham H. Maslow put these life models, phases of life and universal needs into a pyramid for us to study and use.

The pyramid works from the bottom up and illustrates how we graduate from our survival needs to psychological ones. As a lower need is fulfilled, a new and higher one emerges. We climb and climb until we get to the top level of self-actualization.

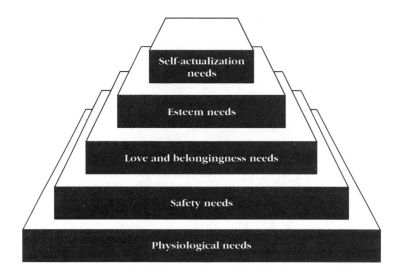

Self-actualized people, according to Maslow, are "happy, mature, self-fulfilled individuals, whose basic needs are met and who are enjoying the fruits of their talents and capabilities and are living to their full potential." Self-actualization is a primary goal for most people, even if they've never heard the term. If *you* want to have a rich, rewarding and satisfying life, you will want to strive for self-actualization. "We all have the drive to want to reach self-actualization," says Maslow, "but we also all possess a fear of growth which often holds us back." Once we are aware of this fear, however, we can *courageously* learn to overcome it.

Life planning requires looking at all parts of your life and needs together. Planning skills help us get our bearings and refocus as often as we need to. Remember, when you don't have a plan, life controls you. Again, when you don't have a plan, life controls you. Mañana is not the time to plan. Today is!

How Latinas Are Held Back

Our Latina cultural messages make it harder for us than for others to reach self-actualization. Why? Because we are predominantly family oriented. We spend almost all of our life's energy bearing children and serving our families, when we should be nurturing our own development as well. This excessive materialism is dominant in Chiquita's cocoon and, unfortunately, allows very little space, time or energy for self-development.

While living in Cuernavaca, Mexico, Maslow worked closely with a Mexico City psychiatrist, Rogelio Diaz-Guerrero. One of their favorite topics of discussion was the nature of femininity and family relations in Mexico versus those in the United States. Maslow was intrigued by the social traits of Mexican women, especially the middle-aged, whom he considered noble. He and Diaz-Guerrero concluded, "Mexican women seemed to become so totally devoted to their families, especially their children, that they lost their spark and became uninterested in the outer world. Middle-class women in North America, on the other hand, strove so hard for self-development that they lost the real pleasures of motherhood and marriage."

One might raise the question, who, then, is better off? Who has a better quality of life? Who has the "choice"? Frankly, we Latinas have so much catching up to do that we have little choice but to spend more time on self-development. We need to improve our status, provide our children with positive role models and beat the poverty trap. How else will we get out of the cocoon?

Because of our proximity to Mexico, relatives and friends come to the United States often. When they come to visit or stay, they bring with them the old traditional culture and customs that resaturate the semiprogressive Latino culture here. The constant influx of immigrants from other Latin American countries does the same. This partially explains why we as a social class have not been able to completely shed the parts of the outdated cocoon from which we would like to escape.

In contrast is the African American woman. Her homeland in Africa is on the other side of the world. The influence of African culture on her life is totally severed because she was forcibly yanked out of her country. Because of loss of contact through slavery practices and geographical distance, the African American woman can't run back and forth to Africa and receives few guests from there. Consequently, she is more assimilated into U.S. society than we are and the African American woman's statistics are a notch higher than ours.

Decisions and Destiny

At what age does one start to plan one's life? How far back can you remember? Do you remember being three, four, five?

When my grandniece Stephanie first heard Linda Ronstadt sing "Por un Amor" ["For Love"], she was barely five. She loved the song and learned to sing it by playing it over and over. Because she knew very little Spanish, she didn't know what she was singing; she just mimicked. If you ask Stephanie, now seven, what she is going to be when she grows up, she says, "A singer like Linda Ronstadt." Stephanie began planning her life the day she first heard Linda Ronstadt sing and discovered her own God-given talent. Linda Ronstadt herself became aware of her destiny when she was barely three, listening to her father's Mexican music.

I knew when I was four years old that I would one day write a book such as this one. Oprah Winfrey, who was reared by her grandmother and got a good licking almost every day "in case she thought of doing bad things," knew by age seven that she was destined for fame and fortune. Awakening to one's destiny can occur at any age. The renowned Julio Iglesias was nearly forty when a serious soccer injury caused him to be hospitalized for months. Informed that he would never be a professional soccer player, he consoled himself with a guitar. To his amazement, he discovered another God-given talent.

Each and every one of you ought to stop to examine any and all interests from childhood on. Ask yourself if you are suppressing interests that may very well hold the key to your destiny.

Remember, however, that being one of the chosen few to have a natural talent or a gut instinct for life's calling does not necessarily mean we reach our destiny in a straight line, without hurdles, curves or obstacles. Life is like a golf course. We play it hole by hole and there is a lot of green to cover.

Don't be alarmed if you don't have any gut instincts about your life's calling. Most people don't. Still, everyone has personal preferences, desires and unique personality characteristics. When these are identified properly, they can steer you to the right career.

Make Each Day Count

A planner is someone who reads, asks questions, jots things down, investigates, searches, gets advice, makes telephone calls, writes letters, thinks and analyzes. Because life is constantly changing, a good planner makes alternate plans and is flexible enough to switch gears when necessary. Learning how to plan means using these techniques all the time until planning becomes a habit. To simplify the process, use this short, easy-to-remember formula:

Stop

Think

Act

"Stop, think and act" in your daily, weekly and monthly activities is applicable regardless of who you are or how you spend your days. A housewife, in order to avoid running helter-skelter, should make a list of her chores and errands. Once she sees in writing what has to be accomplished, she can cluster functions, establish priorities and decide how to get them done efficiently. List making should be a daily habit.

Some folks may dismiss the housewife's duties as trivial, but I don't. During a typical day you might say to yourself: "I have to go to the bank, pay the phone bill, pick up the kids after school, pick up a car part for Ben and go to the grocery store. I must also clean the bathroom and bedroom, call Mother and help Junior fold his newspapers."

A good way to get all of this done would be:

1. Write a check for phone bill. Put in house mailbox.

2. Clean bathroom and bedroom after kids leave for school.

3. Take shower. Get dressed. Pour coffee and call Mother.

4. Go to grocery store. Put away groceries. Fix dinner.

5. Leave the house at 1:30 P.M. Stop at bank. Pick up car part. Be at school by 2:30.

When you make lists, the formula "stop, think, act" becomes automatic. Writing down what you must do makes the chores seem clearer and more manageable. Suppose you don't make a list and do the chores randomly? You'll be running back and forth like a chicken with its head cut off!

If you are a mother with babies or toddlers, you must really stop, think and act. Plan your errands early in the morning, while the kids are rested. Later, when they're napping, tackle what's left. Get a baby-sitter when you have too much to do.

Just as you've planned your day, you can plan your week. I strongly recommend using a purse-size calendar. Make a list of the things you need to do each day and write them down. Stop, think and act! Look at your week. Are you overloaded on Monday and vacationing on Friday? Can you transfer some of Monday's tasks to Friday or to other days? Before you book activities into your calendar be sure to flip the pages back and ahead so you can gauge your energy level. For example, if you are having *la familia* over for an all-day Sunday barbecue, you may not feel up to having a super busy Monday.

Your calendar is your planning guide. Fill in routine commitments such as working hours, class times, exercise and your children's activities. Knowing your obligations ahead of time instantly tells you what blocks of time you have left and makes life much easier. You'll be surprised how much more time you will find in your life just by planning it. The feeling of control is nice too. Knowing what is happening in your life gives you a sense of direction and power. Your decision to say yes or no to new invitations or potential commitments is easier also.

If you are a full-time working woman, planning is critical. Carrying a calendar, an address book and a notebook is a must. You already know about the calendar. The address book is your resource book. List relatives and friends and the names, addresses and telephone numbers of *everyone* you deal with: doctors, dentists, schools, banks, insurance agents, bus company, even your hairdresser. On the blank pages of your book, write down family members' Social Security numbers, driver's license numbers, birthdates and business accounts. Why all this? Because you may need to conduct personal business from your job site. Whether you do it on company time or during your break or lunch hour, having these resources at your fingertips will make things much easier.

The small notebook is for just that, notes. Jot down the things you need to do as they pop into your mind. Write down important things as well as little ones such as: go to cleaners, make hair appointment, buy nylons, get car lubed, or the title of the book you want to buy for Grandmother's birthday. Use it also for recording information, messages or thoughts pertinent to your life that you want to remember.

Housework and the Mamboing Grasshopper

Perhaps the most overwhelming chore for women is coping with never-ending housework. Some readers may feel household chores are unimportant in life planning. They aren't. Unfortunately, women will always be stuck with these tasks. Nonetheless, you must plan housework because you don't want to spend life's precious hours in drudgery. Believe it or not, there are books on how to clean a house. I strongly recommend you buy one! You know how we spend hours in the kitchen? We clean the stove, jump over to the table and then bounce back to the refrigerator like mamboing grasshoppers. Housecleaning books show us how to clean more quickly and efficiently. For example, you should clean your kitchen in only one direction, clockwise, never going back over what you've already done. Following an orderly pattern of cleaning eliminates the time-consuming gyrations we're accustomed to performing. By following the plan outlined in a how-to-clean book, I cut my cleaning time in half. I learned how to make a bed completely from one side before moving to the other side, to avoid more of the grasshopper mambo. The book tells me to equip each bathroom with its own cleaning supplies to avoid unnecessary traveling from bathroom to bathroom, wasting time.

Enlisting children, male and female, to help clean is a must. A chart of rotating chores can keep them on track. Obviously when the children are little, the work gets done slowly. Alone you could probably do it better and in half the time, but the effort pays off later.

A friend of mine has a good theory. She has children and a husband and works full time. Wednesday nights, she cleans her entire house. She says that since she's already tired from work she might as well be really tired, but enjoy a clean house and a free weekend. She says it's easier to get her family to help during the week. On weekends they all seem to conveniently disappear. *¡Orale, Oralia!* ["Way to go, Oralia!"]

Not all of us can clean the whole house in one day or night. I prefer to clean one or two rooms as needed. We have to consider our differences, our individual preferences and personalities.

MOTIVATING MESSAGE

LA QUE NO MIRA ADELANTE, ATRÁS SE QUEDA.
["SHE WHO DOES NOT PLAN AHEAD, STAYS BEHIND."]

12

Success in Life

Know Thyself

Okay, let's do some serious career planning. Find a quiet place where you can do some self-analysis. You'll need a good hour or two, maybe longer, or you may have to do it in several sessions. Start your self-analysis and promise yourself to see it all the way through, for it may be the best investment of time you'll ever make.

You will need a pencil and a large notebook to record your answers to the life-planning exercise. Doing the exercise will help you identify your preferences and lead you to some conclusions as to what you want and don't want out of life. Complete the self-analysis *thoroughly.* You need some real meaning in your life. Spend the time now to find that "special" meaning, based on your preferences, that will make your life significant, help you choose your work or career, and lead you to self-actualization.

Let's go, Chiquita. Here's the first heading for your notebook.

1. **Know Thyself.** Begin with who you are now. Answer these questions and you'll soon know a lot about yourself.

   Who am I? (If this question is too big, answer the rest and come back to it.)

   What special talents and abilities do I have?

   What do I enjoy doing more than anything else?

   What would I do if I could do anything I wanted to?

   What do I want out of life?

   What do I want to be?

   Is what I'm doing now what I want to be doing for the rest of my life?

   What will I be doing in five, ten, twenty years?

   Look around you. What is your environment? Your society?

   Are you happy and thriving in it?

   What changes would you like to make?

2. **List Your Interests.** Think of ten things you *love* to do, then list three ways you could make money doing each one. The surest path to pleasure is choosing work you would like to do for the pure joy of it. Money and opportunity will come if you have the interest and enthusiasm that real involvement brings. Do what you love and the money will follow.

3. **Know Your Own Limitations.** Take physical and mental stock of yourself. If you want to be a police officer or a flight

attendant, could you pass the physical requirements? Do you like to work standing up or sitting down? In noisy or quiet surroundings? Do you prefer working closely with others or independently?

Do you know if you're right brain or left brain? Briefly, but you'll need to do more reading on your own, right-brained people are said to be creative; left-brained, analytical. Since one side is always dominant, knowing which one you are can help you choose a career that's likely to be a natural for you.

Are you left-handed? Would this present a problem in the profession you are seeking? How about your energy level? Can you endure a ten-, fourteen- or sixteen-hour day? Do you thrive on stress or avoid it altogether? Probe your abilities and limitations. Be honest with yourself.

4. **Identify Your Values.** Identify the causes, ideals and beliefs you want to commit your life to. Identify what motivates you. For example, do you seek power, prestige, challenge, money or justice? Ask yourself:

What do I value in being a Hispanic woman?

What are my values concerning children? Should I have them? When? How many? Who will take care of them?

What personal qualities would I like my potential life partner to have? Why?

When is the right time for me to get married?

What are the most important things in my life?

What things are essential in my life?

Who are the most important people in my life?

How have these things and people influenced me?

What cultural messages have affected me most?

What is the meaning of my life?

How do I feel about money? How much money do I need to earn to support the lifestyle of my choice?

How do I feel about nature? About death? About the future?

What value do I place on education, progress, the arts, books, time?

Exactly what am I committed to?

Do I operate from my own attitudes, beliefs and interests or do I copy those of someone else?

Complete this sentence: Before I die, _____

_____

_____ .

The answers to these questions will give you a clearer idea of who you are, your preferences, your interests, your strengths and your weaknesses.

If completing the self-analysis is more than you can handle by yourself and you need help, call the career counseling center at your local high school or community college and look into:

1. Taking a personal development class. These classes last approximately four weeks and are offered at various times throughout the semester.

2. Taking the Meyers–Briggs or Holland personality inventories.

3. Taking the self-administered computerized career programs covering the major aspects of career decision making (including values, interests, skills, educational programs and occupation information).

4. Making an appointment with a career counselor to discuss your unique needs.

5. Spending some time in the counseling center to acquaint yourself with all the resources available.

These services are generally free (or have small fees) and are open to community residents as well as students. Invite a friend to go with you. Call to make your appointments and enjoy a day of self-exploration. You'll have a good time doing it, and the experience will boost your self-esteem and get you started in the right direction. Remember, there is no age limit. With a few exceptions, you can launch into any career if your motivation and desire are substantial, or as we would say, *"con ganas"* ["with desire"].

Aim High, Dream Big

By now you should know your preferences, aptitudes and skills. The next step is to match what you know about yourself with an occupation. As you search, keep the following guidelines in mind:

1. All occupations are oriented by the nature of their duties to people, things or ideas. You should know which of these you lean toward. Concentrate your efforts accordingly.

2. Aim high. Set high goals, particularly if you want to make money. Why be a bookkeeper when you can be an accountant? Why be a baby-sitter when you can operate your own day-care center? Why be a nurse, if you really want to be a doctor? Big dreams beget big accomplishments.

3. No one knows more about a profession than the people in it. Before you get too gung ho about a particular occupation, interview people. Find out all you can. Then judge for yourself.

4. Get experience, paid or volunteer, in your field of interest. Work full or part time. Community colleges offer classes in working at a variety of jobs. These classes offer hands-on experience. Take advantage of these resources.

5. Most well-paying jobs require formal education. Accept education as important as breathing and make it a continuous part of your life. Education, whether it is one or two classes a semester or a four-year term, is an end in itself. It pays off no matter how you do it.

6. College graduates are not the only smart people in the world. Many people educate themselves. How? By read-

ing, listening and observing. A self-educated person is one who could go into business for herself or who takes the initiative and puts in the time necessary to work herself up from an entry-level position to a professional one.

7. Other options in career development include apprenticeships, internships, vocational, technical, trade and home-study courses. Explore these options too.

8. Attend career fairs whenever possible. Ask questions. Gather and study the literature.

9. Assertiveness is necessary in any endeavor. Take charge of your life in your career search. Be persistent, even pushy, if you must.

10. Listen to your gut instincts.

You can make a tentative career choice, but remember you're not stuck with any career for a lifetime! Making a choice allows you to focus on one area. Find out all you can about that particular field. Be assertive here. Ask and risk a little and when you can, a lot. After all, the stakes are high. You are planning *your* life and *your* future.

Here's a "Study of an Occupation" guide to help you.

1. Description
Occupation _____

What is the future for this occupation? _____

What is the beginning, average and maximum salary? _____

What are the hours of the job? _____

2. Job duties
What duties does one actually perform?

_____

_____

What are the related duties?_____

_____

Circle the duties you are most suited to and like.
Would these be interesting and stimulating? _____
(If you answer no, don't go any farther.)

3. Where does one start or enter this occupation?

_____

How does one get promoted? _____
Is the occupation localized or national? _____
Would moving be a consideration? _____

4. What are the requirements in terms of education, training and experience?

_____

Is a license required?_____Type? _____
Are tools, a car or equipment required? _____

5. General information
Benefits?_____

_____

Working conditions?_____

_____

Are there dangers to physical health?_____

_____

Se Habla Español, Inglés y Computadora*

The *Dictionary of Occupational Titles,* available in your library or at your school career center, lists some forty thousand occupations. It is fascinating to browse through this book and see the wide variety of occupations. This variety is what makes life planning so tantalizing. As you look at your choices in the following fields, keep in mind the wise words of John Naisbitt, the author of *Megatrends:* "To be really successful [in the future] you will have to be trilingual: fluent in English, Spanish, and computer."

Here in the next few pages are a thousand occupations. Read through them aloud with a friend or alone. But do it slowly, allowing your mind to enjoy and visualize the excitement of your being in that specific occupation. Circle or mark the ones that interest you. Using your "Study of an Occupation Guide," follow through all the way.

*["Spanish, English and Computer Are Spoken"]

Create a Career
in Fine Arts as a(n) . . .

Actor/Actress
Advertising Copywriter
Archaeologist
Architect
Architectural Restoration
   Specialist
Archivist
Art Dealer
Art Director
Art Historian
Artist
Art Teacher
Art Therapist
Biographer
Book Editor
Book Reviewer
Broadcast Announcer
Calligrapher
Cartographer
Cartoonist
Choreographer
Circus Performer
Columnist
Commercial Artist
Commercial Photographer
Composer
Continuity Writer

Copy Editor
Costume Designer
Critic
Dancer
Dance Teacher
Disc Jockey
Documentary Film Maker
Drafter
Drama Teacher
Fashion Designer
Film Editor
Floral Designer
Foreign Correspondent
Ghostwriter
Illustrator
Industrial Designer
Industrial Journalist
Interior Designer
Jewelry Sample Maker
Landscape Architect
Literary Agent
Lithographic Photographer and
   Process Artist
Magician
Makeup Artist
Merchandise Displayer
Model Maker

Motion Picture Producer
Museum Curator
Museum Exhibit Specialist
Music Director
Musician
Music Librarian
Music Supervisor
Music Teacher
Music Therapist
Narrator
Naval Architect
News Commentator
Newspaper Correspondent
Newspaper Editor
News Photographer
News Reporter
Package Designer
Photo Colorist
Piano Tuner and Technician
Picture Framer
Playwright
Poet
Portrait Photographer
Potter
Puppeteer

Radio and Television Announcer
Science Fiction Writer
Scientific Photographer
Screenwriter
Sculptor
Sign Painter
Silversmith
Sound Effects Technician
Sound and Lighting Technician
Speechwriter
Sports Announcer
Sports Reporter
Stage Manager
Stage Set Designer
Stained-Glass Designer
Stunt Person
Taxidermist
Technical Illustrator
Technical Writer
Television Director
Theater Director
Travel Guidebook Writer
Video-Camera Engineer
Writer

Do You Relate Well to Social Studies? How About a Career as a(n) . . .

Anthropologist
Applied Statistician
Archaeologist
Architectural Restoration
   Specialist
Athletic Coach
Attendance Officer
Case Worker
Child-Care Attendant
Child Monitor
Child Psychologist
City Manager
Clinical Psychologist
College Career Planning and
   Placement Counselor
Counseling Psychologist
Criminologist
Dean of Women
Developmental Psychologist
Drug Counselor
Economist
Educational Psychologist
Employment Counselor
Employment Interviewer
Engineering Psychologist

Flight Attendant
Funeral Director
Geographer
Head of Residence
Historian
Historic Sites Supervisor
Home Economist
Hospital Administrator
Industrial Psychologist
Industrial Relations Director
Industrial Sociologist
Job Analyst
Judge
Kindergarten and Elementary
   School Teacher
Lawyer
Legal Assistant
Management Aide
Marketing Research Analyst
Medical Social Worker
Orientation Therapist for the
   Blind
Personnel Manager
Police Officer
Private Investigator
Probation Officer

Psychiatric Aide
Psychiatric Social Worker
Psychiatrist
Psychologist
Public Relations Worker
Recreational Therapist
Recreation Center Director
Rehabilitation Center Director
Rehabilitation Counselor
Relocation Specialist
Rent Control Hearing Officer
Rural Sociologist
Sales Manager
School Counselor
School Psychologist
School Social Worker
Secondary School Teacher
Securities Sales Agent

Social Ecologist
Social Group Worker
Social Psychologist
Social Security Claims
   Adjudicator
Social Service Aide
Social Studies Editor
Sociologist
Superintendent of Schools
Survey Worker
Teacher of the Blind
Teacher of the Deaf
Teacher of the Mentally Retarded
Teacher of the Physically Handi-
   capped
Training Specialist
Travel Guide
Urban Planner

Translate Your Abilities to a Career in Foreign Language as a(n) . . .

Airline Ground Receptionist
Anthropologist
Archaeologist
Archivist
Art Historian
Bilingual Legal Secretary
Bilingual Medical Secretary
Bilingual Secretary
Bilingual Ski Instructor
Bilingual Teacher
Biographer
Case Worker
College Teacher of Comparative
   Literature
Cookbook Compiler
Customs Inspector
Documentary Film Maker
Editor of Standardized Foreign
   Language Tests
Employment Counselor
Ethnologist
Etymologist
Flight Attendant
Flight Purser
Foreign Buyer

Foreign Correspondent
Foreign Exchange Clerk
Foreign Language Correspon-
   dence Clerk
Foreign Language Editor
Foreign Language Proofreader
Foreign Language Stenographer
Foreign Language Teacher
Foreign Service Information
   Officer
Foreign Service Secretary
Geographer
Historian
Home Health Aide
Hotel Front Office Clerk
Hotel Manager
Import-Export Agent
Intelligence Specialist
International Advertising Copy-
   writer
International Banking Officer
International Broadcast
   Announcer
International Lawyer
International Manufacturer's
   Representative

International Public Relations Worker
International Receptionist
International Relations Specialist
International Social Welfare Agency Worker
International Trade Economist
Interpreter
Lexicographer
Librarian
Management Aide
Missionary
Museum Curator
Music Librarian
News Reporter

Police Officer
Public Health Nurse
Reader
Recreation Center Director
Singer
Sociologist
Translator
Translator of Scientific Documents
Travel Agent
Travel Guide
Travel Guidebook Writer
Traveler's Information Service Worker
Urban Sociologist

Bettina R. Flores

Experiment with the Idea of a Career in Science as a(n) . . .

Aeronautical Technician
Aerospace Engineer
Agricultural Engineer
Agronomist
Air-Conditioning, Refrigeration
  and Heating Mechanic
Aircraft Mechanic
Air Traffic Controller
All-round Machinist
Animal Caretaker
Archaeologist
Astronomer
Audiologist
Automobile Mechanic
Ballistics Expert
Biochemist
Biologist
Botanist
Broadcast Technician
Butcher
Camera Repairer
Cartographer
Ceramic Engineer
Chemical Engineer

Chemist
Chiropractor
Civil Engineer
Construction Subcontract
  Administrator
Dental Assistant
Dental Hygienist
Dental Laboratory Technician
Dentist
Dietitian
Drafter
Electrical Engineer
Electrician
Electrocardiograph Technician
Electroencephalography Techni-
  cian
Electronics Mechanic
Emergency Medical Technician
Engineering Psychologist
Experimental Psychologist
Farmer
Fish and Game Warden
Engineering Psychologist
Fish Hatchery Worker

Flight Engineer
Food and Drug Inspector
Food Scientist
Forester
Funeral Director
Geographer
Geologist
Geophysicist
Health Physicist
Home Economist
Horticulturist
Hospital Administrator
Industrial Arts Teacher
Industrial Engineer
Laboratory Technician
Landscape Artist
Licensed Practical Nurse
Mechanical Engineer
Mechanical Instrument Maker
Medical Record Librarian
Medical Research Librarian
Medical Secretary
Medical Social Worker
Medical Technologist
Metallurgist
Meteorologist
Microbiologist
Mining Engineer
Musical Instrument Maker
Nurse Anesthetist
Nursery Worker
Nutritionist
Occupational Therapist

Oceanographer
Operating Room Technician
Operations Research Analyst
Optometrist
Orientation Therapist for the
 Blind
Orthodontist
Park Naturalist
Park Ranger
Pharmacist
Physical Therapist
Physician
Physicist
Pilot
Plumber
Psychiatrist
Quality Control Inspector
Radiologic (X-ray) Technician
Registered Nurse
Respiratory Therapist
Sales Engineer
School Nurse
Science Fiction Writer
Science Teacher
Soil Conservationist
Soil Scientist
Speech Pathologist
Teacher of the Blind
Teacher of the Deaf
Technical Secretary
Technical Writer
Telephone Line Worker and
 Cable Splicer

Television and Radio Service
  Technician
Tool Designer
Tool and Die Maker
Translator of Scientific Documents
  ments
Tree Surgeon

Veterinarian
Vocational Agriculture Teacher
Watchmaker
Wildlife Specialist
Wood Technologist
Zoologist

As you investigate these and other fields, be sure to find out the availability of jobs in the future. My niece Rachel, thirty, read in the *American Almanac of Jobs and Salaries,* available in your library or career center, that the demand for physical therapists is projected to increase by 42 percent. She's a machine operator now, but she is retraining herself to become a physical therapist. She will spend five years in college while she works at night. Before she made her decision, Rachel went through all the steps in this chapter—self-analysis, personality inventory, career counseling and a study of occupations. She talked with physical therapists and studied Maslow. With *mucho gusto* she is looking forward to a secure, self-actualized future.

It is also important to compare wages. Below are average salaries for some occupations. Cost of living rates in individual cities affect the figures.

Physician	$108,000
Lawyer	$ 88,000
(private practice with experience)	
Engineer	$ 43,000
Architect	$ 36,000
Nurse (RN)	$ 27,000
College Librarian (master's degree)	$ 26,000
Truck Driver	$ 25,000
Electrician	$ 24,000
Secretary	$ 18,000
Cosmetologist	$ 17,000

Why not get political too. One of the best and fastest-growing occupations for college-educated women will be to work as members of the U.S. Congress or state legislatures. Congress now pays about $133,600 per year. State legislatures pay up to $57,000. Both have excellent benefits.

Let's also include the many other roads to fame and fortune. How about sales—real estate, auto, insurance, stocks or bonds. There's the world of entertainment—writers, producers, movie stars and musicians. There are more and more female athletes. The inventors of popular fad items like the Hula Hoop, pet rock and wacky wallwalkers often hit it big. Most significant of all, consider the female entrepreneurs of Mrs. Fields cookies, Carmelita's restaurants, Heidi's frozen yogurt, Ramona's tortilla factory, Estée Lauder cosmetics, Vera scarves and textile designs and oh, yes, the woman who created billion-dollar Barbie, Ruth Chandler.

Having It All

If you use life-planning skills, you're bound to be more successful than the person who doesn't. Success in life can mean different things to different people. It can mean cooking the Christmas tamales in one hour, getting through high school, becoming a U.S. citizen, being a good wife and mother, getting an average job, becoming an engineer, politician, teacher, nurse, doctor, lawyer or even a writer.

Each of us has a personal thermometer for measuring success. There is absolutely nothing wrong with wanting it all—success, health, wealth, love and happiness. You'll be more apt to have it all when you know what you want and are willing to risk, work and sacrifice to accomplish your goal. If you still have doubts, tape this message to your mirror:

> "There is truly no difference between women who are successful and those who aren't," says Maria Nemeth, Ph.D., at the University of California, Davis. "It is not a matter of skill, ability or knowledge. Women who are successful *do it!*"

Are we serious about all this? You bet we're serious!

Now is the time to do this planning and take your personality inventories. *Now! Today!* ¡Ahora! *Call! Do It! Go!*

MOTIVATING MESSAGE

CHIQUITA'S OLD CULTURE	CHIQUITA'S NEW COURAGE
MAÑANA	NOW!

Tomorrow

In the new millennium, the evening space shuttle to Moon Station Mesa is filled with excited Earth commuters looking forward to their four-day weekend.

Alicia and Alan, married ten years, discuss their timetable for finishing the house-illuminating project they started two weeks ago. Alicia is working outside; Alan inside. Alicia prefers doing the outside because she can practice her mariachi songs in the moon air and because she enjoys bouncing from area to area in her stylish, iridescent moon suit. Alan wants to do the inside to catch the big Earth versus Moon football game on the robot television set that will follow him around as he works. Sharing the work means they will be finished by Saturday night, leaving Sunday and Monday free.

Like new lovers in ecstasy, Carlotta and Pedro are contentedly sipping moon margaritas. They spent their day on Earth shopping for baby clothes. Married six years, they expect their first baby next month. They plan to have only two children—a plan that coincides with their investment and their dream to own two homes, one on Earth and one on the moon, since Carlotta wants to leave a property inheritance to each child. Carlotta says to Pedro, "Let me see our savings balance again." Pedro raises his wrist, punches in a code and the wrist computer flashes a report of their holdings. Carlotta opens the heart locket she wears around her neck, verifies Pedro's figures on it and smiles. Happily she says, "All our hard work and education have really paid off."

On the eighth level of the space shuttle commuter, Carolina and Christina, roommates since their freshman college days and now both Ph.D's, compare notes on the moon college's criteria for their second Ph.D.'s. Carolina has a slew of credentials. She works as a consultant and is in demand for her expertise in spaceology and multicultural family living. Christina, a space physicist, has a collection of outstanding awards for her discovery of micromoon elements essential for growing food. Her work keeps her mostly in a laboratory, but her writing keeps her traveling around the globe and solar system. Both are well educated and financially set for life. Their only worry is how to fill their lives with more challenges, which is why they each plan to get another Ph.D. in a completely new field.

On the ground level of the commuter, the noise is almost deafening. Many children of different ages and races run around as happily as if they were in their own homes. In the background, multicultural music plays loudly, a stream of Japanese, English, Chinese, Italian and Latino sounds. On this flight and deck, the fathers are always in charge. The mothers attend classes of their choice—spaceaerobics, meditation, body beauty or educational programs.

The dinner bell sounds and the fathers automatically dump their beers and scurry to fasten children into their seats. As the children scramble to order, a tiny Latina girl and a Latino boy collide and begin to fight over who pushed whom. The little boy, unwilling to discuss the matter, punches the girl in the stomach and she dramatically clutches herself in pain. Hardly a second passes, though, before she grabs his arm and wrestles him to the floor. She climbs on his back, sits on him solidly and with all her strength twists his arm until he cries, "I give up!"

The father comes to break them up and says to Juanito, "You'd better have more respect for our señoritas. The old ways are gone forever."

"*Sí,*" says the little girl. "*¡Basta!* Enough!"

How I Found My Wings

*I*t's true. I left home when I was twelve.

I answered a newspaper ad for a mother's helper. Two phone calls and one hour later, I made the move that would change my life forever.

It didn't take much. I telephoned the lady who placed the ad and she called Mother Superior, my Catholic school principal, for references. Within the hour, this stranger was parked in our front yard, waiting to take me to her home where I would help out with three small children.

Taking a cardboard suitcase with my few belongings, I enthusiastically jumped into her car and waved good-bye to my mother. I didn't even know where I was going. I didn't care. I wanted out.

There were no tears or protests from my mother. I did not cry. I didn't hurt my mother. If anything, I relieved her burden by leaving. What she as a welfare widow could provide and what I wanted were incompatible. Somehow we both understood this.

That day, I became an emancipated child with the determination to take care of myself.

I'm sure I didn't know what I wanted or what I was looking for back then. What child would? I did know, however, what I had wasn't it. I knew I had to search for my dreams elsewhere or be trapped forever in the west side of Fresno, California.

I despised my pretwelve life mostly because it was boring. Eating potatoes and beans every day didn't cause me any real suffering. Working in the fields—tomatoes, grapes, cotton—and cutting peaches was hard work, but I liked the spending money it gave me and I had no choice. Having to wear the same school dress five days in a row was embarrassing, but then it was for the other girls too.

No. I despised my childhood because life's drudgeries overwhelmed everyone. There were no adventures and few discussions regarding personal ambitions. Worst of all, there was no hope of change. Each year the seasons came, the seasons went. We existed by reacting to everything around us, year in and year out.

I don't mean to paint a bleak picture. Most of the time I was a happy little girl. I played with dolls and dishes. I played cowboys and Indians. I traded comic books on Saturdays. I roller-skated around the government-subsidized complex until dark or until I was dragged indoors. I went to the playground every day during the summer, where I participated in arts and crafts, folk dancing, water ballet and nearly every sport. I chased boys. They chased me. I had a best friend named Irma. I slept at her house; she slept at mine. We borrowed each other's clothes. We went to the movies and dances together, got into trouble together.

My most precious times, however, were spent alone, lying in the poppy fields between the shacks, dreaming myself away under the promising blue skies with the energetic wind snapping in my face.

Nonetheless, I wanted something to happen. Maybe I wanted someone or something to disrupt the routine with "Hey, I got a new car!" or "We're moving to San Francisco. Isn't it exciting?" or "You've got to read this book. It's great," or "Let's make plans to go to the snow on Saturday," or, even, "Let's drive to the other side of town to see what it looks like."

I must have had the urge to move early in my childhood, because I was always curious about the other side of town. Whenever anyone with a car came over, I was the first to say, "Let's go for a drive."

It seems I was always observing the behavior of my older sisters and brothers. I don't know why. They did normal things like go to school, to work and to mass. I watched my sisters with their boyfriends. When I disapproved of their choices I told them so and why. He's too short. He's not smart. He doesn't have a job. Of course, hypnotized by teenage romance, my sisters never listened to me. My mother never knew of their boyfriends because they sneaked out for their escapades. They had to. One time my mother caught one sister and went after her and the boyfriend with a long hard stick. Both of them got it good. Another sister was what we called "*terca*" ["stubborn"], and she ran away from home a lot. My poor mother thought she had failed her.

My two brothers seemed untouchable. I couldn't say anything to them. I don't know why, but most of the time I was too scared to even look at them. I guess they were too superior, too macho.

Life, I would say, was pretty normal. It was I who needed and wanted change. And here it was!

My new employer lived in Fig Garden, then a prestigious

section of town. I remember driving through what is known as Christmas Tree Lane and thinking that she was kidnapping me. I believed that beyond Christmas Tree Lane there was no residential development, no civilization. Suddenly frightened, I thought the worst—my body would be found later in some remote field and at the same time the fear hit me, so did the guilt. I could just hear my mother saying, *"Te dije"* and *"Por vaga."* ["I told you so. This is what you get for being restless and a wanderer."] But, of course, my imagination was running away with me and everything was fine.

My new environment was mind-boggling. The luxurious house, cars, money, entertainment and especially the variety, amount and quality of the food were incredible! This seemingly self-indulgent quality of life was almost beyond comprehension to a twelve-year-old from Poorsville.

Was I impressed? Of course. I was also furious. *Furious!* I was furious that people could have so much more than they could ever use or even need while *we,* who lived just ten miles away, had so little, had nothing! It wasn't fair, I told myself. They frivolously threw away what we would thankfully cherish. Their lives were self-fulfilling, plentiful, exciting and planned; ours were poverty-stricken, self-sacrificing, uneventful and unplanned.

Much of this fury is still in me today. My real concern was *how* did they achieve such a quality of life? What prompted them to pursue such advantages? Was this lifestyle handed to them or what? What place in the working world provided such amenities? How could I get some of them?

I loved my five-dollar-a-week job in Fig Garden. The three kids and I went to Catholic school together. My duties were to make sure they did their homework, had clean uniforms, polished their shoes very white, made their lunches and said their bedtime prayers. When they played, I played. After all, I was still a kid myself. Once my employer asked me to do some ironing. I guess she thought I was going to be one of those Super-Latina domestics, so I made sure her blouses stayed wet and wrinkled and she never asked me again.

I must have looked pretty ragged because one day she took me shopping. Actually, she took me for a makeover: haircut, manicure, facial, clothes and shoes. The hairdresser said I had baby-fine hair and slyly asked if I was Spanish. I said, "No, I'm Mexican." This became my pet peeve. The barrio girl stood ready to punch anyone who referred to *her* as "Spanish."

After my first year as a mother's helper, I moved on to another family, another mansion, then to another family, another castle, until I graduated from high school.

To this day, I still crave change because with it comes excitement, new risks, more adventures, new people, new places and new ideas.

Change is the essence of life. Have you ever seen a butterfly come forth from its cocoon? It doesn't simply leap free and fly. It struggles slowly, pausing time after time. And when it emerges, its body is still in the shape of the cocoon. Gradually the wings unfold and the butterfly moves them, drying them in the sunlight and fluttering them tentatively until it startles itself with momentary flight. Hastily it grabs the cocoon again, clinging and waiting. And then, miraculously, there comes the moment it knows it can fly and it lets go of its cocoon and floats away in the sunny fresh air.

And you, too, Chiquita,
          can emerge from your cocoon,
               trust your wings,
                    and fly . . .

Suggested Reading

Education, formal or informal, is one of your best companions in life. When all else seems to fail you—your own energy, family, friends, the system—education is there like a lifelong source of fresh air. Education helps you to learn, to be a free thinker, to be independent, to be creative and to understand the real meaning of life. Education is what brings one of age. A delightful pathway to education is through reading. Make reading a habit throughout your life.

This bibliography is in sections to help you read according to your interest. Most of these books, fiction and nonfiction, can be found in your library or bookstore. If they are unavailable, you can request that they be ordered.

Women's Studies

Bird, Caroline. *Born Female.* New York: Pocket Books, 1968.

De Beauvoir, Simone. *The Second Sex.* New York: Alfred A. Knopf, 1952.

Dowling, Colette. *The Cinderella Complex.* New York: Pocket Books, 1981.

Edwards, M., and E. Hoover. *The Challenge of Being Single.* New York: Signet Books, 1975.

Estés, Clarissa Pinkola, Ph.D. *Women Who Run with the Wolves.* New York: Ballantine Books, 1992.

Friday, Nancy. *My Mother My Self.* New York: Dell Books, 1977.

Friedan, Betty. *The Feminine Mystique.* New York: Dell Books, 1963.

Friedman, Sonya. *Men Are Just Desserts.* New York: Warner Books, 1983.

Goldstein, Daniel, Katherine Larner, Shirley Zuckerman, and Hillary Goldstine. *The Dance Away Lover.* New York: Ballantine Books, 1977.

Hite, Shere. *The Hite Report.* New York: Alfred A. Knopf, 1987.

Hulst, Dorothy J. *As a Woman Thinketh.* California: DeVorss & Co., 1982.

Norwood, Robin. *Women Who Love Too Much.* New York: Pocket Books, 1985.

Psychology, Inspiration, New Age

Bristol, C. M. *The Magic of Believing.* New York: Pocket Books, 1948.

———— and H. Sherman. *TNT: The Power Within You.* New York: Prentice-Hall, 1954.

Butler, Pamela. *Talking to Yourself.* New York: Stein and Day, 1981.

Carnegie, Dale. *How to Stop Worrying and Start Living.* New York: Simon and Schuster, 1971.

————. *How to Win Friends and Influence People.* New York: Simon and Schuster, 1937.

Dyer, Wayne. *Your Erroneous Zones.* New York: Avon Books, 1976.

Hill, Napolean. *Think and Grow Rich.* New York: Fawcett, 1960.

Kassorla, Irene C. *Go for It.* New York: Delacorte Press, 1984.

Lerner, Harriet Goldhor. *The Dance of Anger.* New York: Harper & Row, 1985.

MacLaine, Shirley. *Out on a Limb.* New York: Bantam Books, 1983.

Maltz, Maxwell, M.D. *Psycho-Cybernetics.* California: Wilshire Book Company, 1960.

Mandino, Og. *The Greatest Salesman in the World.* New York: Bantam Books, 1968.

Maslow, Abraham H. *Toward a Psychology of Being*. New York: Van Nostrand Reinhold, 1968.

Murphy, Joseph. *The Amazing Laws of Cosmic Powers*. New York: Prentice-Hall, 1989.

Ostrander, Sheila, Lynn Schroeder, and Nancy Ostrander. *Super-Learning*. New York: Dell, 1979.

Naisbitt, John. *Megatrends*. New York: Warner Communications, 1982.

———. *The Year Ahead*. New York: AMACOM, 1984.

Peale, Norman Vincent. *The Power of Positive Thinking*. New York: Walker and Company, 1985.

Ponder, Catherine. *The Dynamic Laws of Prosperity*. California: DeVorss & Co., 1985.

———. *The Millionaire from Nazareth*. California: DeVorss & Co., 1979.

———. *Secret of Unlimited Prosperity*. California: Book Graphics, 1981.

Ross, Ruth. *Prospering Woman*. New York: Bantam Books, 1982.

Viscott, David, M.D. *Risking*. New York: Pocket Books, 1979.

Ziglar, Zig. *See You at the Top*. Gretna, La.: Pelican Publications, 1974.

All About Us

Anaya, Rudolfo A. *Bless Me, Ultima*. California: Tonatiuh International Inc., 1972.

Galarza, Ernesto. *Barrio Boy*. Indiana: University of Notre Dame Press, 1971.

Lewis, Oscar. *The Children of Sanchez*. New York: Random House, 1961.

Martinez, Al. *Rising Voices*. New York: Signet Books, 1974.

McWilliams, Carey. *North from Mexico*. New York: Greenwood Press, 1968.

Meier, Matt S., and Feliciano Rivera. *Dictionary of Mexican-American History*. Westport, Conn.: Greenwood Press, 1981.

Mirandé, Alfredo, and Evangelina Enríquez. *La Chicana*. Chicago: University of Chicago Press, 1979.

Ortega, Phillip D. *We Are Chicanos*. New York: Pocket Books, 1973.

Padilla, Amado M. "Hispanic Journal of Behavioral Sciences," Vol. 4, No. 2, 1982.

Peterson, Frederick. *Ancient Mexico*. New York: Capricorn Books, 1959.

Portilla-Leon, Miguel. *The Broken Spears*. Boston: Beacon Press, 1962.

Rendon, Armando B. *Chicano Manifesto*. New York: Macmillan, 1971.

Rodriguez, Richard. *Hunger of Memory: The Education of Richard Rodriguez*. New York: Bantam Books, 1982.

Simmen, Edward, ed. *Pain and Promise: The Chicano Today*. New York: Signet Books, 1972.

Simpson, Lesley Byrd. *Many Mexicos*. Berkeley: University of California Press, 1971.

Steiner, Stan. *La Raza: The Mexican Americans*. New York: Harper & Row, 1969.

Sowell, Thomas. *Ethnic America*. New York: Basic Books, 1981.

Vasquez, Richard. *Chicano*. New York: Avon Books, 1970.

Villarreal, Antonio José. *Pocho*. New York: Anchor Books, 1959.

Miscellaneous

Andreason, Nancy C., M.D. *The Broken Brain*. New York: Harper & Row, 1984.

Campbell, Jeff. *Speed Cleaning*. New York: Dell Books, 1987.

Gandhi, Mohandas K. *Gandhi: An Autobiography*. Boston: Beacon Press, 1957.

Locke, Steven, M.D., and Douglas Colligan. *The Healer Within*. New York: Signet Books, 1986.

Suggested Reading

Mitchell, Margaret. *Gone with the Wind*. New York: Macmillan, 1936.

Stone, Irving. *The Passions of the Mind*. New York: Doubleday, 1979.

Stone, Jeff, Jane Meara, Maureen Kelly, and Richard Davis. *Growing Up Catholic*. New York: Doubleday, 1985.

————. *More Growing Up Catholic*. New York: Dolphin Books, 1986.

Workshops, Lectures, Author Appearances

Chiquita's Correspondence

If you find *Chiquita's Cocoon* to be helpful and informative and would like to consider taking a seminar with Bettina—or if you would simply care to share your response to *Chiquita's Cocoon* with her—please feel free to write her at the following address:

Bettina
P.O. Box 2037
Granite Bay, CA 95746-2037
(916) 791-2237

Please indicate whether your letter can be used in workshops, lectures or subsequent books. Bettina will make every effort to answer your letter. *Chiquita's Cocoon* is available in Spanish. If your local bookstore does not have the Spanish version, you can ask the store to order it; this is a free service. Ask the store to stock extra copies . . . for the next Chiquita.

ABOUT THE AUTHOR

BETTINA R. FLORES is a freelance journalist, educator, and public speaker whose work has appeared in both English and Spanish magazines and newspapers. She received the 1991 Latina Author of the Year Award for her self-published edition of *Chiquita's Cocoon* and is frequently referred to as the Betty Friedan for the Latina woman. Bettina Flores lives in Northern California with her husband, an attorney, and their four children. She is currently writing a workbook to accompany *Chiquita's Cocoon*.